Nov 16

PRAISE FOR
DRINKS
BY ADAM MCDOWELL

"A thoroughly useful and enjoyable compendium of drinking lore and knowledge, with an ample dose of much-needed cynicism, too often lacking in books of this type."

—PHILIP GREENE, cofounder of
The Museum of the American Cocktail and author of
To Have and Have Another: A Hemingway Cocktail Companion

"There is, as yet, no perfect user's guide for life. But for the many moments in our lifetimes when a decent drink is required—whether it's a crisp pilsner on a summer afternoon, a glass of champagne on a special day, or a dry martini when the clock strikes five—Adam McDowell's *Drinks: A User's Guide* has you covered."

—PAUL CLARKE, executive editor of
Imbibe magazine and author of *The Cocktail Chronicles*

"If you don't know how to drink, this book is for you. If you do know how to drink, this book is also for you, since everyone is sure to be charmed by Adam McDowell's sage and friendly advice about what to order, in any setting. After years of tweaking his philosophy of drink, McDowell has finally shared his accumulated knowledge in this invaluable resource. Not since Kingsley Amis has reading about drinking been this much fun."

—CHRISTINE SISMONDO,
author of *America Walks into a Bar*

DRINKS

A USER'S GUIDE

■ ■ ■

ADAM McDOWELL

with illustrations by
KAGAN McLEOD

A TARCHERPERIGEE BOOK

tarcherperigee

An imprint of Penguin Random House LLC
375 Hudson Street
New York, New York 10014

Most TarcherPerigee books are available at special quantity discounts for bulk
purchase for sales promotions, premiums, fund-raising, and educational needs.
Special books or book excerpts also can be created to fit specific needs. For
details, write: SpecialMarkets@penguinrandomhouse.com.

Library of Congress Cataloging-in-Publication Data
Names: Mcdowell, Adam.
Title: Drinks : a user's guide / Adam McDowell.
Description: New York, New York : TarcherPerigee, 2016.
Identifiers: LCCN 2016023526 (print) | LCCN 2016032155 (ebook) |
ISBN 9780143111269 (hardback) | ISBN 9781101992760 (ebook)
Subjects: LCSH: Alcoholic beverages. | Cocktails. | Beer. | BISAC: COOKING /
Beverages / Wine & Spirits. | COOKING / Beverages / Bartending. | COOKING
/ Reference.
Classification: LCC TX953.M33 2016 (print) | LCC TX953 (ebook) | DDC
641.2/1—dc23

Printed in the United States of America
10 9 8 7 6 5 4 3 2 1

Book design by BTDNYC

FOR EMILY

■ ■ ■

CONTENTS

PREFACE:
BECOMING A
COMPLETE DRINKER

The art of rational drinking is an accomplishment as indispensable as dancing or bridge. . . . To know how to drink is as essential as to know how to swim, and one should be at home in both these closely related elements.

—FRANK MEIER, BARTENDER AT THE
PARIS RITZ, 1936

HAVE YOU EVER NOTICED that characters in old novels and movies seem to know exactly what to drink and when? Many of us can only look back in envy at a time when people would simply know which brandy or champagne was the best to kick back with in the midst of some European adventure or could spontaneously fix up a tray of gin rickeys like Tom Buchanan does in *The Great Gatsby* or had some idea how to tell whether a martini was well made.

We're paying more attention to these details lately because we live in the dawn of a new golden age of drinking. Indeed, we can realistically hope it will turn out to be *the* golden age of booze. The general quality of wine is improving, product selection in virtually every category of beverage is increasing, craft distilleries flourish, old cocktail recipes are being rediscovered and new ones invented, cities that once featured two decent cocktail bars now have fifty jockeying for your attention, and the vogue for tasty craft beer rises like a froth with each passing year.

Meanwhile, for most of the public, this is all a little terrifying: It means there are more choices to make than ever before, and it's difficult to know how to cope with it all.

I know this because I talk to people about drinks all the time. I've written about booze for a major Canadian newspaper called the *National Post* for more than a decade, and over the past few years I've been popping up on a daytime lifestyle program called *The Social* to chitchat about beverages and try not to spill things on live television. You might do a hundred different things with your life, but if you write and broadcast on the subject of drinks, it's pretty much the only thing people will want to talk with you about at parties. And when people find out what I do, their first instinct is usually to apologize for what they're drinking. They say they feel silly because they don't know anything about wine. Or they mime a defensive gesture like turning their beer label around so I can't see it, lest I judge their peasant ways. This tells me that people know they could probably be drinking something tastier or more exciting, but something's stopping them from finding out what it could be.

If we are to enjoy the golden age of glorious drinking that is upon us, we must shed these defensive gestures, because being shy about drinks relegates us to retreating to the same old foxholes, sticking to what's familiar. Instead, we ought to be curious about the new world in front of us, ready to courageously advance into unknown territory.

If you are holding this book, I hope it's reasonable of me to assume that you thirst (as it were) for more knowledge. What you'll find is that people who know a thing or two about drinks are usually only too happy to share. You're at little risk of being ridiculed by those who truly know their stuff. At least in my experience, applicants to the fellowship of drinks geekery are welcomed with open arms and flowing bottles.

Aim to learn enough about drinks to become what I think of as a "complete drinker," someone who has a rough idea of what there is to drink, what these things taste like, and the right situations and means for serving them. To set yourself on that path, be willing to take an exploratory sip of (just about) anything. It sounds daunting but isn't nearly as tough as some people—whose motives I will leave you to guess at—are keen to make it look. Just think of alcohol the way you think of food: a field to explore in search of what you personally find delicious.

The trouble is people don't know where to begin this journey, and until now I didn't have the proper tools to help them. There are books about rum and gin and beer, books about bitters, many books about wine, and so on. (Websites, too, naturally.) Yet I've often wished I could point people toward a general handbook for everyday drinking. There wasn't anything up-to-date that really fit the bill—the late Kingsley Amis's *Everyday Drinking* was the closest thing, and something of a bible to me personally. But it's rather British and published so long ago that it contains references to £6 bottles of champagne and such. To my great surprise there really wasn't a more suitable, recent, and semicomprehensive book on the market for people who want to know what to drink during particular occasions, how to prepare and serve these things, and how to avoid feeling like an ass while doing so. So I decided to write one.

Even if you don't proceed through this volume in a straight line from cover to cover, you can treat it as a resource for the adventure I've just outlined. Each chapter ahead is a dunk in one of the many pools you'll encounter in the drinker's life, offered with the hope that they'll give you enough encouragement to dive in and swim.

I dwell longer on the topics that I feel deliver an especially rewarding experience as well as on the ones (such as whiskey) for which more information is necessary in order to help you feel you're on solid footing. You may think I've given wine short shrift—I just figure it's an easy subject on which to find advice—and I've avoided certain topics entirely (cider, punch, dessert wine) because I think you can get by without a lot of instruction at first. The idea wasn't to cover absolutely every aspect of drinks, but to give you the best push that I could based on what I've figured out over the years.

With cocktails, meanwhile, I've mainly stuck to vintage recipes, but contemporary ones are built on the same principles. If you follow the instructions herein, you ought to be able to attempt any recipe under the sun: They really aren't as complicated to make as you may fear, and mastery of a few simple techniques is enough to make you reasonably competent.

Note that the concepts of *everyday drinking* or being a *complete drinker* do not entail having something in your hand at all times. Far from it. If you care for moderation, it will care for you. And you may find that drinking better leaves you satisfied with drinking less.

It's also worth noting that the aim isn't to turn you into a know-it-all or a snob, as I think people sometimes expect from a lover of booze. I promise you can keep being your old self. As the Zen master Wu Li counseled, "Before enlightenment, chop wood and carry water. After enlightenment, chop wood and carry water." In other words, if you're truly enlightened, it's enough that you know it yourself. You'll have no desire to go around trying to prove your enlightenment to anyone else, and they shouldn't notice a big change in you—other than that you choose better wine and throw better parties.

Another lesson from the Buddhist scriptures, of all places: A guy gets hit with a poison-tipped arrow. He refuses to let anyone pull it out until he finishes asking a litany of questions. What's the name of the man who shot it? What village does he come from? And so on. The injured fellow croaks before anyone has a chance to yank out the toxic shaft. When it comes to alcoholic beverages, knowledge can be a valuable thing, but focusing on trivia can be the poison arrow that sucks the life out of a party.

It all distills down to this: Drinking is supposed to be fun. People always want me to share insider tips, little gems I've pocketed about drinks over the years. This realization is the most precious by far: In any conflict between enjoying the moment and obsessing about the drinks, the moment must win out. Pay attention to the people and conversations around you first. The drinks remain your distant second priority.

DRINKING
IS SUPPOSED
TO BE FUN.

A FEW HOUSEKEEPING NOTES

Like an obnoxious barfly I admit I do repeat myself. While this book is a new project, certain turns of phrase and indeed whole sentences and recipes are lifted from my writing over the years, especially my columns in the *National Post* and a blog that is now long defunct. Sometimes you explain something as well as you're ever going to on the first attempt.

I've tried to make this book as universal as I could manage, but my own cultural experiences and dialect may soak through. It simply can't be helped that I come from Canada, an obscure Commonwealth realm known for its exports of uranium and lamentable pop singers.

Liquid measurements for cocktail recipes are in American units because cocktails are American, and even most of us raised in metric countries will usually think in ounces when mixing and stirring.

The terminology for milk and cream at different fat percentages varies by country to a surprising degree. Certain sugars change names from country to country as well—for instance, powdered sugar, icing sugar, and confectioner's sugar are all the same thing. I've done my best to help you navigate this kind of thing but I apologize for any lapses that send you madly a-Googling.

PART I

■ ■ ■

ORIENTATION

Some Dos and Don'ts for the Savvy Drinker

The dipsomaniac and the abstainer are not only both mistaken, but they both make the same mistake. They both regard wine as a drug and not a drink.

—G. K. CHESTERTON

I T'S AN UNFORTUNATE FACT that mastering the art of boozemanship involves learning how to dodge rip-offs, rudeness, and nonsense. Most people are ignorant about drinks and therefore susceptible to misdirection. Others—the scoundrels!—see potential gain in exploiting that general ignorance. Knowledge and experience make the artful drinker impervious to bullshit and instill in her the confidence to insist on whatever beverage she actually wants and will enjoy in the moment. Here I provide some general guidance on avoiding the usual pitfalls of everyday drinking—advice for a world in which the art is halfway lost, but well on its way to being regained.

DOs

Approach Drinking as a Culinary Endeavor

Having the right approach to drinking means you don't set out to get drunk any more than you would dine with the intention of getting full to the point of vomiting. Puking is losing, either way.

Nature may take its course when you have a few and you may find yourself a little wobbly and slurry, and life will probably go on (more or less) as it was. But deliberately setting out to get intoxicated is a foolish idea, and I don't think I actually needed to tell you that anyway.

_____

DRINK MINDFULLY.

_____

Treating drinks the way you treat food means doing it for the company and for the flavor—the aromas, the texture of drinks. *Drink mindfully*. It may sound absurd, but try it, and I'm sure you'll agree that concentrating on what you're drinking and going slowly, with moderation, leads to better results than shots and chugging.

The culinary drinking principle also means you should try new things all the time, just as you ought to do with cuisine. Don't be afraid of novelty; explore the unfamiliar. If you don't like something, no big deal. Don't finish it. Try something else.

To fear new drinks, as I know many people do, is to lock oneself into certain patterns and habits. This leads to absurdities like quaffing cold Mexican lager when it's snowing outside or drinking warm red wine on a hot patio: in both instances, it's far from the optimal drink for the occasion.

You don't just keep eating all the things you ate at twenty-two years old and only those things. By the same token, if you drink only your go-to pale lager or that same cheap Aussie wine every week, isn't it kind of the same thing as eating only instant ramen noodles?

To become a complete drinker, try different beverages in an attempt to suit the mood and the climate you find yourself in. Match the food you're eating; that's the really important one. You should aim to find yourself something to eat while you drink, and your refreshments should taste right with what you're eating— each bite enhances the sip that follows, and vice versa, without clashing. There's plenty of guidance on how to seamlessly match food, drink, and occasions in reputable books (including this one), magazines, and the behavior of the locals in Old World cultures.

Mind Your Manners at the Bar

Behave yourself. For example: You push up to the bar to wait your turn. Next to you is a fellow in a blue hat, already waiting. Bartender comes over and looks at you to get your order. What to do? Gesture at the man in the blue hat. "He was here first, then it's me," you say. This is basic bar etiquette.

Never Be Rude to Servers and Bartenders

Politeness counts. Snapping your fingers, being gruff, not minding your pleases and thank-yous: None of these behaviors makes you look good to anyone worth caring about. In all realms of life, it's the worst people who pick on those who are restricted in some way from standing up for themselves. You should judge severely, and, frankly, avoid, anyone who treats servers poorly.

Grab the Corner of the Bar on a Date

If you can, snag the corner spot. If you and your potential paramour are sitting side by side, you won't get a chance to look at each other—or touch knees, if things are going well.

Stop Drinking When It's Time

The very instant you start to feel wobbly, push your glass/cup/beer bong aside. Same goes the moment you realize you're just no longer having fun. There's already more hooch in your system on its way, so it's best to cut off the supply at once. When looking out for friends and others, loud speech is actually a worse sign than slurring, and repetition is worst of all: It's a tipoff that the brain is positively swimming in alcohol . . . swimming in alcohol . . .

swimming in alcohol. Get a repetitive drunk home by whatever safe and legal means you have available.

USE FRESHLY SQUEEZED JUICE AND FRESH ICE IN COCKTAILS

Always choose fresh. Pouring prebottled lemon or lime juice from the grocery store into a drink makes it unfit for human consumption. The chapter on bar gear tells you how to squeeze your own lemons, limes, and oranges. Putting old ice that stinks of fish sticks into a guest's beverage is an exit application from civilized society altogether.

EXERCISE SPECIAL CAUTION AROUND CARBONATED DRINKS

Watch out for the bubbles. If something fizzes, it gets you drunk faster than a flat beverage of the same strength. (One exception: Beer doesn't seem to hit too quickly.)

ORDER FANCY COCKTAILS

You may not be too familiar with the fancy cocktails on the menu, but how will you ever find out what they taste like if you don't try them?

I know people sometimes hesitate at the prices, too, but cocktails at a nice bar will tend to include 2½ to 3 ounces of liquor, sometimes more (sometimes a *lot* more in New York or New Orleans). If you do the math, you'll find that cocktails are usually the best value proposition on the drinks menu. Let's imagine a very nice bar in a big city, where Manhattans cost $15. That's 2 ounces of whiskey and 1 ounce of vermouth, so call it three small drink units. If you ordered three whiskey and sodas at the same bar, it might cost you $18 (if you're lucky), and the result wouldn't be nearly as tasty and interesting. Savvy drinkers choose cocktails for the sake of bang for the buck alone.

SEND BACK A DRINK THAT ISN'T RIGHT

It's okay to send back a poorly made drink; this practice keeps everyone honest. When I'm *certain* (not guessing) there's something wrong with a drink—it's an underpoured pint,* a beer that tastes off (like butterscotch, for example, a sign of diacetyl contamination), a cocktail that tastes like it wasn't made properly, or, in the classic case, a wine that tastes quite flat and lifeless (and is therefore likely "corked")—I'm content to send it back, and I won't take any guff about it. You might have to politely stand your ground. Saying, "I'm sure you want me to be happy with my drink" tends to work.

DON'Ts
DON'T GENDER DRINKS

There's no such thing as a man's drink and a woman's drink.

The easiest way to demonstrate that you don't know a damn thing about drinks is to repeat silly rote notions about which things are for boys and which are for girls.

Ribbing your male friend who orders a bloody Mary or giving a backhanded compliment to the woman who drinks cognac straight from a snifter is wrong on a few levels. You're not doing your friends any favors if you're implicitly making them second-guess their choice of beverage. Can't a person enjoy a swig in peace?

---

* In most English-speaking countries, a pint is 20 ounces by law. If they call it a pint, that's how much beer they have to give you; less is cheating. Suspiciously small glasses are a common trick, especially in Canada. In the United States, pints aren't an everyday beer-serving format, but a pint, if that word is explicitly used, should be 16 ounces.

Aha, you say, What about wines and other products with aimed-at-women names like Mommy Juice and such? Well, that's a trick question: This sexism in liquid form is not for women or for men, nor is it fit for any human. It's for pouring down the drain. Ditto any product with an overtly dudely name.

Nor are there young person's drinks and old person's drinks. Professionals in the world of drink—winemakers, writers, critics, sommeliers, servers, and so on—regard this sort of nonsense as outdated and naïve.

In short, gendering drinks just makes you look like a jerk. So does saying this or that drink should or should not be consumed by members of a particular class, nationality, race, and so on. All drinks are for all adults who want to try them.

Don't Believe Anything Anyone Tells You About Drinks

Treat every boozy factoid as an urban myth until you confirm it somewhere reliable. Drinks-related chatter is riddled with marketing lies, misconceptions, and hand-me-down misunderstandings. I've identified some examples in these pages, but because I can't cover it all, my advice is to generally be on guard when a person or ad or clickbait website tries to persuade you on some factual point about drinks. Nonsense flourishes unchecked in our midst. Doubt everyone, including me—while I stand behind the approaches to drinking discussed in this book, bear in mind that every right way is someone else's wrong way.

Don't Say *Mixologist*

I don't personally have a problem with the term *mixologist*, which has a deeper pedigree than you might imagine (it's from the mid-nineteenth century). However, mixologist and mixology are so contentious and unloved among the cocktail cognoscenti that it's best to avoid them. Bartender or (in some countries) barman will do just fine.

DON'T DRINK THE WINE AT WEDDINGS

Wine is nearly always bad at weddings. Meanwhile, the spirits at the bar are all the popular ones, of the same quality as ever. Focus your efforts there.

DON'T FALL FOR THE "BEER BEFORE LIQUOR" MYTH

You know how it goes: "Beer before liquor, never sicker. Liquor before beer, you're in the clear." Like most things that sound like a schoolyard rhyme, it doesn't seem to be true (if you want to test it on yourself, be my guest; don't say I didn't warn you).

Also don't say, "I heard [blank] prevents hangovers." Many of us have wished for a magic hangover preventative. You can keep wishing. The scientific literature on this subject is as extensive as it is inconclusive. The only sure way to avoid a hangover is not drinking. That, or being constitutionally hangover-proof, as certain lucky people are.

DON'T SAY, "LET'S DO A SHOT"

Shots are usually a terrible idea, especially at the end of the night. Do you really want to be super drunk for the cab ride home? My rule on speed drinking is to never instigate chugging or doing shots. But as with beer in a bucket—also usually a bad idea—if someone else initiates the round, I grin and bear it. Better to go along than get in the way of other people's fun. Order something wiser when it's your turn. Lead by example.

Don't Say, "Let's Order Bottle Service"

Thinking about bottle service? Stop right there because you're about to get suckered. Bottle service is a massive scam. They charge you an arm and a leg for ordinary spirits (yes, Grey Goose is ordinary) and make you prepare them yourself with boring mixers, like cola that's rapidly warming and going flat. They don't even give you the tools you need to make a decent cocktail. There you are, drinking vodka and orange juice like a college kid at a house party. How does anyone think this is a premium experience?

Don't Fear Drinks with Egg in Them

Egg whites have little to no flavor themselves, so drinks made with them will not taste like egg. The egg is for texture, not flavor.

People also hesitate to order drinks with eggs because of fears over salmonella. It might help to know that the U.S. Food and Drug Administration estimates that these harmful bacteria infect just one egg out of twenty thousand in the United States. That's a big number; it would take you fifty-five years to consume twenty thousand eggs at a rate of one a day.

If you have a compromised immune system or a food intolerance, avoiding raw egg is probably a wise precaution, fair enough. For the rest of us: You can't have a Ramos gin fizz, a pisco sour, or a number of other tasty drinks unless you're willing to run the risk.

Don't Drink When You're Upset

If you're in a foul mood, go for a walk. Take a bath. Meditate. Save the drink for a time when you'll enjoy it.

PART II

HOW TO DRINK BEER, WINE, AND SAKE

DRINK INTERESTING BEER (AND SHUT UP ABOUT IT)

They who drink beer will think beer.

—WASHINGTON IRVING

CHOOSING BEER HAS BECOME a bit political, in a way that few would have predicted twenty years ago. The world is probably going to force you to decide what kind of beer drinker you are—whether you're game for the diversity (and challenge) of craft beer or you prefer to stick to the solidarity, simplicity, and safety of the mass-market brands. It has even been suggested by certain commentators that beer snobbery is crowding out good pub conversation—the idea being that pubgoers are talking about beer instead of gabbing entertainingly about weird things that happened to them on the train or about art or politics.

We're talking about beer here, not life and death, so maybe we ought not to take it so seriously. But this has become a situation in which one must take sides, and the way I see it, people who have a beef with craft beer are wrong.

The argument that you need to drink bland beer in order to converse with your friends is as dumb as saying you can talk over a cheese plate only if the cheese came out of a cellophane sleeve. I call bullshit on the notion that you can't talk about your day with a fancy-pants IPA or saison in your hand. I've done it plenty of times.

I much prefer my argument, which is simply that a

PEOPLE WHO HAVE A BEEF WITH CRAFT BEER ARE WRONG.

world in which beers taste different from one another is a better world than one in which they all taste the same. Only by embracing craft beer can we live in that world.

Craft beer is not supposed to be about snobbery—and when snobbery does happen, it's not fair to blame the inanimate, delicious beer. The alternative, which the big brewers served up to us in many countries for decades, was the same bland flavors over and over again.

I am, however, in favor of pub conversation. Don't talk about your beer for more than a few seconds at a time. ("How's that one?" "Terrific, goes well with the curry." And so on.) Talk with your companions about art and politics and weird things you witnessed on the train. For centuries beer has served as a fuel for conviviality, and that remains its rightful role. If your pals just want to yammer on about their beer—or worse, express their disdain for yours—it's not time for different beer, it's time for different friends.

There are even occasions when I'm quite all right with drinking mass-market, generic beer. When fishing or assembling patio furniture or helping a friend move, watery beer can taste just right. And obviously if someone just hands you a Pabst Blue Ribbon you say thank you and drink it. Anything else would be rude.

Otherwise, a person should enjoy different kinds of beer just like a person should enjoy different kinds of cheese, simple as that.

A Beer for
All Seasons

Such power hath beer. The heart which grief hath canker'd
Hath one unfailing remedy—the tankard.

—CHARLES STUART CALVERLEY

BEER IS SUPPOSED TO BE EASY. Kingsley Amis
observed that serving beer is as simple as getting it cold
enough, then asking your guests, "Who's not for beer?"
and then subtracting the number of raised hands from the number
of guests in your party.

While I won't ruin the simplicity any more than I have to, the
variety of beer is now far greater in most places than it ever was in
the past, making the beer aisle more of a challenge to navigate.

To decide what beer to drink, try to match it to the food and
season. You'll usually find that hot weather and light food calls for
lighter-bodied beer and blustery weather and heavier food matches
better with heavier beers, which can be (but aren't always) dark in
color. What follows is a calendar of beers to drink by season.

EARLY SPRING

If all you've ever consumed is mass-market lager, follow my advice
when spring hits and fill the fridge instead with **pale ale**. It's a
fairly broad term and a misleading one, since many pale ales are
relatively dark in color, down to ruby red (the "pale" refers to pale

malt, a lightly kilned barley that forms the basis of the beer). Pale ale takes many forms and differs from country to country—an English pale ale tends to be maltier than an American one, which will usually be more bitter, and you expect a Belgian one to be stronger and more complex than the other two. For a quick round-the-world tour of drinkable middle-of-the-road brands, you could try Fuller's London Pride (UK), Sierra Nevada Pale Ale or Anchor Liberty Ale (USA), and Palm (Belgium). Find one you enjoy that seems to go with a lot of different foods—as pale ales tend to do—and you've got a go-to beer for the season, or indeed for the year. You could drink a lighter, English-style pale ale with just about anything. (Incidentally, we're not talking yet about *India* pale ale, or IPA, here. That's a different animal; see "Autumn.")

Meanwhile, if you order a pint of **bitter** in England, it probably won't actually be all that bitter tasting. *Bitter* is just the British

ALE VS. LAGER

Lager is typically crisp tasting, light bodied, and fermented at ice-cold temperatures with yeast that sits at the bottom of the fermentation vat. Ale is fuller tasting and fuller bodied and is fermented at cellar temperature (around 50°F/10°C) by yeast that prefers to float on top. While most of the *volume* of the world's beer is lager, most of the *diversity* is found in ales. Bottom-fermented, crisp, cold-brewed lager got the upper hand over ale largely thanks to the advent of refrigeration—which made it easier to make—and it never really looked back. The craft beer revolution of recent years has allowed ales to regain some of their former territory, but I'd wager that just about one in twenty beers quaffed around the world is an ale, and the remaining nineteen are lagers.

term for pale ale on draft, and most of them are not bitter at all compared to the average craft-brewed American pale ale. Light bodied, earthy, and low in alcohol—often down in the three-point-nothing range—they make terrific beers to down one after another in what beer lovers call a "session," thanks to their overall mildness.

Oh, and speaking of **mild**, that's actually the name of a positively ancient form of English beer—so ancient that it's probably the closest extant style to the beer Shakespeare would have known. Deep brown, low in alcohol (again, 3% to 4.5% is fairly typical), and malty-sweet, you could almost think of it as bitter's darker-complexioned and much older cousin. Shame it's nearly extinct. It's been unpopular since something like the 1920s. In fact, writing in 1949, George Orwell used mild in a scene in *Nineteen Eighty-Four* as an example of a beer an old man would reminisce about. Mild can still be found, however, especially in its native England and Wales.

The Germans, meanwhile, drink a strong lager called **bock** in the springtime to make the transition from the heavier beers of winter. A bock is a German style of strong lager that takes its name from the billy goat. There are several subspecies within the bock genus, including one called **maibock**, whose name specifically calls for it to be drunk in the month of May.

Some bocks are winter beers, many are for spring, but, frankly, no one's going to make sure you're observing the difference so just grab what you can. Just know that a **doppelbock** (that is, double bock) will be quite high in alcohol—above 7% is typical—and an **eisbock**, or ice bock, may well lay you flat if you go overboard on it. Maybe save that one for winter, when you're somewhere safe and warm with soft furnishings for you to pass out on.

My favorite bock is Doppel-Hirsch Allgäuer Doppelbock. Sour grapey-winey flavors give it a dry, fruity tingle, nicely balanced against the right amount of bitterness in the hops. The label may bear the violent image of stags bumping antlers, but it's a lover, not a fighter—a beer very much at peace and in harmony with itself. (We can forgive Hirsch for putting pictures of deer on the bottle when, as you now know, they're really supposed to be goats.)

LATE SPRING

As mild weather turns to hot, we look to warmer climes for inspiration. Kudos to the Americans for coming up with **cream ale**, a crossbreed of ale and lager. A cream ale is technically an ale, as the name suggests, but one that's hopped and cellar aged so that it comes out crisp, like a lager. Genesee Cream Ale is probably the best-known brand Stateside, while Canadians will recognize Sleeman Cream Ale. Beer snobs don't necessarily think too highly of cream ale, but if you serve it with sausages and/or hot dogs and potato salad, no one will complain, not even the snobs.

Meanwhile, two other cream ale–like beers are perfect for the warmth of late spring. **Canadian ale** and **Aussie ale** are unofficial terms that recognize the fact that Canadians and Australians are fond—possibly to an unreasonable degree—of ales masquerading as pale lagers. They're essentially cream ales but more bitter. Examples: Molson Export remains a top-selling beer in much of Canada (though Molson Stock Ale is tastier), while Labatt 50 ("Fitty") enjoys a cult following in Ontario and Quebec. In Australia, a call for a "VB" means ice-cold Victoria Bitter.

Finally, like cream ale, **kölsch** is an easy-drinking crowd-pleaser that also goes down nicely with tube-shaped meat. It's from Cologne, Germany, and I imagine washing down sausages is what it was designed to do. Kölsch is an Old World product and is often made by small North American breweries. This all means that unlike cream ale, kölsch actually enjoys some cred among the beer geeks, in case that's important to you.

Lambic beers make another lovely choice for springtime, especially as a dessert. Only the Belgians seem capable of really executing lambics (though there are American homages called **wild ales** if you care to try), and that's largely because lambics are a terrifying hassle to brew. Normally a brewery monitors its microorganism population like an Arizona border guard, but a good portion of the fermentation for lambics is performed by wild yeasts and bacteria that blow into the brewery through open windows. The resulting beer is refreshingly sour, and that sensation is usually offset by the addition of fruit. Cherry, raspberry, and blackcurrant are common, though there is at least one banana lambic, by the brewer Chapeau.

Gueuze (pronounced sort of like GOOD, but with a *Z* instead of a *D*), meanwhile, is what a lambic is called if unflavored. Cantillon makes a terrific one. Gueuzes have been compared to drinking vinegar; pair with French fries.

SUMMER

Speaking of sour beer styles, you can't shake a rake at a hipster beer bar these days without knocking over a glass of **saison** (sez-AHN). That's French for "season," and the name refers to the beer's history as a summer thirst quencher for farmhands in Wallonia.

Farmhouse-brewed ales are a strong tradition elsewhere in Belgium and France; a **bière de garde** or **farmhouse ale** could be very much like a saison and will at any rate be a thirst-quenching beer intended for summer drinking, despite its high alcohol percentage. Beer writer William Bostwick called it the Gatorade of the 1800s. Unlike Gatorade, saison may contain barnyard-like aromas. The farmer brewers of two centuries ago would have followed practices intended to prevent stray yeast and bacterial strains from landing in the beer and creating off flavors. But they were totally ignorant of microbiology, so the beer would have turned out a bit funky. Contemporary brewers of saison will sometimes deliberately add eccentric microorganisms to the batch and let them do their thing. The sour character of many saisons makes them delicious with fermented foods, such as pickles and sauerkraut. (Other tasty matches: combinations of starch and cheese, such as poutine, sausages, burgers, and roasted poultry.)

The gold standard among brands is pale, yeasty Saison Dupont; it has many imitators of varying quality. Among North American examples, Goose Island Sofie is a good place to start. Be warned that many saisons are high in alcohol—Dupont is 6.5%, for example—without necessarily tasting like they are. You can't just pound saison all night.

A **pilsner**, for example, makes a lighter-tasting summer beer option. Of all the traditional beer styles, this can seem the most familiar. It's a light-colored, crisp central European lager, the template on which most of the world's giant beer brands were based, from the Americas to Asia to Africa. Though pale lager is planet Earth's default beer type now, a beer this clear and clean tasting was new and exotic in the 1840s. A young Bavarian brewer named Josef Groll invented pilsner beer for his employer, the Czech city of Pilsen, which of course lent its name to the brew, a pale, light-bodied, and bitter style of lager.

To me there are two kinds of pilsner. First there are genuine

---

HOPS

Some people believe beer is brewed from hops, but that's not the case: Beer is brewed from barley, often wheat, and sometimes other grains and starches. The hops are there just to add flavor to the beer, and they act as a natural preservative. (It's the cones of the plant that are harvested and used in beer, by the way.) A lot of the spicy, herbal aromas in beer come from hops. Sometimes tropical fruit flavors, too. There are dozens of hop breeds for brewers to choose from; my favorite one to say is fuggle. The more famous and relevant ones include cascade, Citra, and saaz.

---

ones, mostly from Germany and the Czech Republic. They sport a grassy and herbal tang thanks to a generous addition of hops, but remain easy drinking. Then there are big-brewery imitators that taste like nothing.

Pilsner (real pilsner) really does work in a lot of situations thanks to its relatively unobtrusive flavor. Sip on a pilsner while you're paddling a boat, cooking burgers, or whatever other happy-go-lucky activities would make your winter self jealous.

Pilsner also does a terrific job of clearing away fat and salt thanks to the crispness and the hops, so keep it in mind if you're stuffing your face with fries or corn dogs or popcorn. As for brands, my favorites are Radeberger and Bitburger from Germany, and Golden Pheasant from Slovakia.

For a little twist on patio drinking, go for German- and Belgian-style pale pale and cloudy wheat beers. The German **hefeweizen** and Belgian **witbier** (or Belgian white beer) are both light and refreshing with a middling 5% or so alcohol content. They match with quite a lot of foods and, like pilsners, don't need to be overthought. You will need to decide whether to add the squeeze of lemon (I don't), but other than that just sit back and enjoy a foamy pint that may contain flavors of banana, clove, bubblegum, and citrus. In the case of the Belgian and Belgian-style white beers, there is usually added orange peel and coriander. Be careful when you pour these and other beers that are bottled "on lees," meaning they have a layer of white sludge at the bottom. That's spent yeast and grain protein, and while it's not harmful to consume, the beer will taste better if you can pour a glass without disturbing the sediment. Store the bottle upright in the fridge so the white stuff settles at the bottom, not on its side, and it will be easy to pour a clear glass of beer later.

AUTUMN

As the air turns crisper and the food heavier, the beer should deepen to match the weight. Enter **India pale ale**, darling of beer fanatics. IPA, as it's known, is almost synonymous with the craft beer movement, at least in the United States. American (or West Coast–style) IPAs are characterized by a tropical-fruity and sometimes shockingly bitter bouquet of hops.

Alas, the quest for bitterness has become something of an obsession in the arcane arms race of New World IPAs, to the detriment, I think, of craft beer and its reputation. If you can believe this, grown men actually brag about the International Bitterness Units (IBUs, to those in the know) of the IPAs they've tried. Brewers play along by making beers that are far too bitter for a typical palate to really enjoy. If there's a pun on "hops" in the name of the beer, it's likely to be pretty extreme, bro—proceed with caution. The whole one-hop-manship contest is certainly a distraction from the task of making delicious beer. I encounter relatively few North American IPAs that are enjoyable enough to order a second one, though there are exceptions. Even if you're game, many IPAs are a bit like heavily tannic Cabernet Sauvignon: You need to pair it with food, lest your tongue be overwhelmed. The extra bitterness comes in handy when you're sampling some of the fattier foods of our stuffed-crust times. IPA often matches well with braised meats, stews, curries, and poutine or anything else covered in cheese and/ or spices and/or has "stuffed" in the name.

India pale ales originated not in India but in England, though they were indeed intended for sale in India back when it was part of the British Empire. The beer was brewed extra-strong and extra-hoppy in order to survive the long boat ride without spoiling. IPA has made an interesting journey over the course of its history, one that beer writer Pete Brown relates in surprisingly engrossing fashion in his book *Hops and Glory*.

If you're celebrating Oktoberfest, you'll of course need to get yourself some **Oktoberfest lager**, which is simply a medium-bodied lager that's a little darker and heavier than pilsner. If you can find it, start with Hofbräu Oktoberfestbier. The very image of a strapping Teutonic lager, it's blond, disciplined, and strong (6.3%). Serve Oktoberfest lager in steins, and it should nicely wash down bites of sausage, sauerkraut, schnitzel, and other German and central European foods.

When you start to feel the icy hand of winter approach, pre-pare by reaching for darker beers, which will tend to be "maltier" (that is, sweeter). I find myself mostly reaching for beer that's darker than copper after mid-October. In my house, when the clocks go back, the beer turns black.

Returning to Germany, many of its wheat ales and lagers have a dark side. Look for **dunkel** on the label, which means "dark"; these beers can be surprisingly light on their feet, which makes them appropriate for the transitional weeks. Take Weihen-stephaner Hefeweissbier Dunkel, a dark wheat beer. It starts with a molasses-like sweetness, but without the roasted flavors that turn some people off darker beers. This is surprisingly clean and light bodied for a dark beer, finishing with a cleansing but not overwhelming bitterness.

Other situations where dark lagers shine: Try a dark Japanese lager (such as Asahi Black) with ramen, or a dark Mexican one (Negra Modelo, for example) with chili con carne. Meanwhile, a tall glass of Köstritzer Schwarzbier is the emperor of **dark lagers**. Legend says this stuff kept Goethe alive for a while, but who knows.

While other mammals think of hibernation, the passing of each November makes me want to seek out Schneider Aventinus Eisbock, a dark Munich wheat beer that's downright chewy and molasses-like, with a foamy and creamy texture. It harmonizes splendidly with many one-pot meals.

Other beers to look out for in late fall are a little more obscure. Belgian siblings **oud bruin** and **Flemish red ale** are sour and

CASK ALE

Most draft beer is served from kegs, which use gas for carbonation and as a source of pressure to push the beer through the line and into your glass. With kegged beer, the yeast has been filtered out, and any stray remaining specimens are dead. In some places, especially England, beer fans go gaga for old-style casks, which use manual pumps instead of gas pressure to pull the beer through the lines. In a cask beer, the yeast is still alive and the carbonation is naturally present. The bubbles are a byproduct of yeast consuming the sugars in the beer. So the CO_2 (carbon dioxide) is yeast farts, essentially, and sooner or later you'll encounter pub dwellers who revel in beer that teems with yeasty life.

complex. As an example of each, seek out Duchesse de Bourgogne and Rodenbach. Certain darker, brooding ales from the British Isles, namely, **barley wine**, **wee heavy**, and **scotch ale**, are likewise complex and make terrific beers for the fireside. Traquair House Ale, brewed in an old manor house, is a beautifully raisiny and woody wee heavy; that's a Scottish ale style invented by people who obviously know what it's like to stare out the window and sigh on a blustery November day.

WINTER

I come from a part of the world where everyone complains about winter. But me? I just smile, because winter means **stout** and **porter** are back. (What's the difference between them? Long story short: nothing.)

Though probably invented in England, stout/porter is often associated with Ireland thanks to the global popularity of Guinness. I have nothing against Guinness; it's quite good for a mass-produced beer (and if you ever get a hold of the Guinness brewed in the company's Nigerian brewery, grab it; it's exquisite—that's an old beer geek secret). But if you enjoy Guinness, know that there are many stouts and porters out there, most of them superior. Go out and explore them.

Stout pairs beautifully with snowy days. And with oysters, which are at their freshest and enjoy the widest availability in winter. During the Victorian era, common folk in the British Isles lapped up oysters and stout, an unpretentious delicacy that fit a humble budget on a special occasion. Eventually the habit faded, and once again it was Orwell who noticed; his 1944 phrase "a pleasant little whiff of oysters and brown stout" was meant to call to mind a sentimental vision of the Victorian age. I'm happy the pairing—I can't explain why it works, but it does—has been revived of late. There are even "oyster stouts." Some are simply sweetish stouts that a brewer feels would go especially nicely with raw mollusk; oyster stout is just a pairing suggestion in that case. There are indeed stouts infused with oyster, but I'm less alarmed by that than another trend: As with IPA, there's been a tendency in recent years for craft brewers to push stouts and porters into extreme flavor territory at the expense of the kind of balance that works in an actual meal. Too often, beers bearing the descriptors "imperial," "Russian," or "Baltic" are the product of more enthusiasm than prudence and may contain sufficient aromas of burnt coffee and motor oil to put off all but the most die-hard extreme beer fans.

If strong flavor is what you want, I would steer you instead toward **abbey** and **Trappist ales.** They're highly regarded and quite strong, typically 8% alcohol or higher, and if you're used to quaffing regular-strength beer they can hit you like the Holy Ghost. Enjoy these beers with friends over a winter feast, slowly, and you'll be fine. Drink them like wine, by the measured glass.

All Trappist beer is made in one of eight European monasteries, by monks of the Trappist order. Seven of these sites are in Belgium or in neighboring regions of the Netherlands and France. The last Trappist monastery that makes beer, Stift Engelszell, is located in Austria and started brewing beer only in 2012, so (stage whisper) it's not really considered part of the club.

The Trappist monasteries vary in their production capacity and enthusiasm for commerce. Unless you live in Antarctica, you could probably put this book down and sniff out a bottle of Chimay within ten miles. On the other hand, if it's Westvleteren you want, maybe look into flights to Brussels.

Thank God for secular brewers, then, who have stepped in to create "abbey ales"—the term refers to a beer in the Trappist style, but not made by monks. (That doesn't mean they can't also be monastically delicious.) Many abbey beers and other strong Belgian ales are given "sinful" or sinister names to distinguish them from the work of monks. Hence Belgium's Duvel (Devil), Inferno, and Malheur (Misfortune) and Canada's La Fin du Monde (The End of the World) and La Maudite (The Damned).

Whether holy or secular, strong Belgian ale comes in various strengths: **dubbel** (double) tends to be dark and roasty; a **tripel** is a strong pale ale, drier than a dubbel and with a bouquet of interesting aromas; and a **quadrupel** will tend to be quite powerful indeed (say, 10% alcohol) and almost chewy in its dense complexity. There is not really such a thing as a single, by the way; although the monks reserve a weak beer for their own table and people sort of half-jokingly apply the term to that stuff. You can't ever buy this, except sometimes at the monastery itself. To make things even more complicated, some of the monasteries don't use the dubbel-tripel system. Orval makes just one beer, a relatively light tripel-style beer, and Rochefort simiply does its own thing and gives its beer numbers (6, 8, and 10—a tally of how many commandments it's likely to make you break, perhaps?).

To end our year of beer, I'll suggest you mark December 31 with Chimay Grande Réserve. For some reason it's known as just Chimay Bleue when it comes in a smaller bottle. Either way, the Chimay with the blue label is one of the world's classics. There was a great beer critic named Michael Jackson (no, no, no, different guy—this one was big, white, and British) who called Chimay the world's most port-like beer. His tasting notes included thyme, pepper, nutmeg, and sandalwood. Even if your impressions are just "This beer tastes a little like chocolate and a little like wine," it's all well and good if you enjoy it.

WINES FOR
EVERYDAY DRINKING

Wine cheers the sad, revives the old, inspires the young,
makes weariness forget its toil, and fear her danger, opens a
new world when this, the present, palls.

—LORD BYRON

Y OU'VE COME TO THE WRONG BOOK if you're
looking for advice on how to spend piles of money on the
world's great wines, which vintages of Bordeaux are optimal for stuffing your cellar with, and that sort of thing. I'm more
about helping with your shopping list than your bucket list.

There are many people out there just dying to give you advice
on the big Cabernet Sauvignons, the pricey Chardonnays, and the
perfect Pinot Noir—which most of us might splurge on a couple of
times a year—but the pressing issue is actually what to do this
evening. What will taste right with dinner? What will make you
want to stay out on the porch and keep sipping away? What
should you bring to that party?

Most of the world's wine is bought and consumed with
thoughts like this in mind. The ins and outs of everyday wine
drinking are easier to master than comprehensive connoisseurship,
and knowing a smart buy or two to pick up on the way home for
dinner makes a bigger impact on our day-to-day lives than remembering which are the best vintages of an expensive wine like Burgundy or Barolo.

That's important to bear in mind for those of us in countries that really discovered wine only in the latter half of the twentieth century. Wine drinking has been on the rise for decades in Britain, the United States, and Australia. The English-speaking world—which hardly consumed wine before the 1950s—is slowly getting into the habit of serving the stuff with dinner, as has been done in Catholic Europe since time immemorial. (Meanwhile, Asia's turn appears to be next.)

What I think is holding back nontraditional wine-drinking cultures from adopting the gift of the grape as a natural and casual part of a weekday dinner is this lingering suspicion that we might be doing it wrong. There's an irrational fear that unseen sophisticates are lurking behind the curtains, looking down their noses at our choices.

I get that wine criticism is intimidating. I write about the stuff as part of my job and I'm constantly overwhelmed by how much there is to know. The immense diversity and confusing terminology of Italian wine alone can leave my head swimming. Others feel completely comfortable here. For some people it's just plain interesting to snoop around the nooks and crannies of wine lore, just as it's fun to learn about whiskey or beer or stamps. Who am I to knock a harmless and enjoyable pursuit?

But for the rest of us—whose knowledge of wine will always be limited and practical—you ought to know, first of all, that wine enthusiasts aren't all that snooty, at least in my experience. In our time it's not considered cool to be undemocratic about drinks, and real-life wine lovers are like any kind of geeky enthusiast: They're pleased to find out someone new is performing the necessary initiation activities of sampling and reading. If you're new to wine and you're attending tastings or asking questions of sommeliers and the staff at your local wine bar, I'm sure you're already discovering that you're being welcomed into the fold, not pushed away. You can't run afoul of the wine police because there is no such thing.

Meanwhile, if you're not that interested in knowing everything about wine, you don't have to. Just learn as much as you need to know, and keep drinking the stuff. (See my tips on choosing wine in the pages that follow.) Alexander Pope said a little learning is a dangerous thing, but when it comes to wine, a little learning may be precisely the right amount. A little learning may be all you have time to internalize or all you can remember when it's quick-decision time at the wine shop. Many of the good people who work in the wine world would hasten to agree that you don't need to have memorized the difference between Côte de Beaune and Côte de Nuits in order to enjoy a glass of red Burgundy. But it's useful to know that Pinot Noir is the grape used to make it.

WHEN IT COMES TO WINE, A LITTLE LEARNING MAY BE PRECISELY THE RIGHT AMOUNT.

As for matching food to wine, there's a lot of talk today about not overthinking it. Some radicals in the wine world even suggest you just drink whatever with whatever. I personally prefer to eat red meat with red wine, reserving white wine for seafood and poultry. Call me conservative, but it works. Bucking the old rules requires a knowledge and a skill with wine that most of us do not possess.

This is the secret to everyday wine drinking: Keep going. Keep learning. Keep trying wine until it doesn't seem like a stranger at the table. Figure out what you enjoy, and how you like to enjoy it.

How to Drink
Great Wine on a
Cheapskate's Budget

'M NOT ONE OF THOSE people who claims that expensive wine is a total scam. Certain people insistently blog that you should just stick to Two-Buck Chuck (Charles Shaw, the cheapo California wine sold at Trader Joe's in the United States) and stuff that comes out of a Tetra Pak because everything else is a pretentious rip-off. This kind of talk is just clickbait and misguided anti-elitism. Pricey wine is often worth it, and that's what the next chapter of this book is about.

But you can't always afford the top-shelf stuff. You need alternatives. Even among less expensive wines, there's usually a noticeable gap in quality between the best and the worst. There are plenty of reasons to learn what's what and not just grab the cheapest thing at random.

The aim is to find wines available in your region and at your budget that you can put on the table on a weekday and feel good about, even if a friend pops over. As someone who buys and drinks wine regularly while trying not to spend too much, here's what I have learned about drinking well for cheap.

Be Wary of Cartoon Animals and
Obviously Gendered Packaging

Don't buy anything that seems to be trying too hard to appeal to a novice, or to men or women exclusively. What you want is wine that was primarily meant to chase the savvy-but-bargain-conscious European grocery store shopper. What your average Frenchman does not buy is wine with an animal mascot. Such a wine might be good or might not be fit for humans; it's dinner roulette. Meanwhile, a sassy name often (though not always) means the wine is vile plonk. Exercise caution. In nature, bright colors can be a warning that an organism is toxic. If you buy a wine with a label that's trying too hard to be cute, expect to be poisoned.

Don't Look to the Americas or the Pacific for Everyday Bargains

Wines from Australia, California, and other regions outside Europe can be fine in the middle to upper end, but the economics of those areas doesn't encourage quality wine to be produced cheaply. That means no Two-Buck Chuck, sorry. For rock-bottom bargains, your best wager is wines from Europe, specifically the Mediterranean—countries where most adults drink wine every day. This creates a competitive market for great wine at bonkers price points, and the entire world benefits. My weekday dinner wines tend to come from Spain and Italy, and one of these days I'll do the homework to learn more about the options from Portugal and Greece.

Learn a Little About Grapes and Regions

If the wines you enjoy come from Europe, particularly Italy or France, you might want to learn how to identify wines by the region or style, not by the name of the grape. Producers in EU countries are often legally barred from telling you which grape(s) are in the bottle. They use "appellations" like Beaujolais and Brunello di Montalcino, the purpose of which is to protect regional monopolies (the practice also reflects European notions of *terroir*, a concept that refers to the way things like microclimate and soil quality supposedly contribute to the flavor profile of the finished product). A Chablis producer, for example, cannot legally tell you on the label that the wine is made with Chardonnay grapes. You just have to know—and it's worth learning. If you discover at a wine tasting that you enjoyed the bold blackberry of a Nero d'Avola, you'd want to know that you'll find many of the tastiest, best-value examples labeled Terre Sicilane IGT (see the "What Grapes Are in There?" box).

I know. Most of us don't like homework. But since there's no test, you can learn at whatever pace works for you and stop when you feel you know enough to identify the wines you find especially tasty.

Heed the Advice of the Wine Critics Working and Publishing in Your Country or Region, Particularly When You're Just Starting Out

People with far more knowledge and experience than you and I regularly taste wines at all price points, and are in a position to know when a $10 bottle could pass for a $20 one. Start with their recommendations.

Notwithstanding the second point, readers in the United States, Australia, and Canada will be able to find high-quality wines made domestically that don't cost too much in the home country (though they can end up on the expensive side when exported). Wine critics in your own country will have pointers on which ones deliver value for the dollar.

Try Lots of Cheap Wine

What do you have to lose? If you don't like one bottle, cook with it and open another. And if you're playing the field, sampling lots of different wines, it's useful to have a few wine stoppers in the kitchen drawers so you can stretch a bottle for a few nights (it's a good idea to refrigerate the wine meanwhile, especially if it's white).

Look for Wines That Are Light and Tend to Be Consumed Young

. . . which are generally properties of the wines I'll discuss in the rest of the chapter.

DO THE RATINGS MATTER?

In 1977, the American wine critic Robert Parker issued his first newsletter, using a 100-point scale to rate wines. Easy to understand and widely imitated, the 100-point system eventually be-

WHAT GRAPES ARE IN THERE?

Somewhat confusingly, certain wine styles, especially European ones, can be coy about what grape varietals are actually in the bottle. If the back of the label doesn't give you any hints, the big word on the front might.

Barolo, Barbaresco (Italy): made with the complex Nebbiolo grape

Beaujolais Nouveau (France): Gamay Noir

Red Bordeaux (France), known as claret in British English: made with some combination of Cabernet Sauvignon, Cabernet Franc, Merlot, and (in lesser amounts) Petit Verdot and Malbec

White Bordeaux: Sauvignon Blanc and Sémillon in dry wines; other grapes (e.g., Muscadelle) in sweet wines

Red Burgundy; called "Bourgogne" in French: Pinot Noir

White Burgundy: Chardonnay. Chablis is really dry Chardonnay from northern Burgundy

Brunello di Montalcino, Vino Nobile di Montepulciano, Chianti (Italy): made with the silky Sangiovese grape

Meritage (North America): made with Bordeaux grapes in the United States or Canada

Red Rioja (Spain): Tempranillo, perhaps blended with Grenache

White Rioja: Viura

Pouilly-Fumé and Sancerre (France): Sauvignon Blanc

Primitivo (Italy): a grape varietal, but it's helpful to know that some DNA tests have strongly suggested that Primitivo—a bold grape that lends wines lots of juicy berry and pepper aromas—is actually the same thing as red Zinfandel, grown in California and elsewhere

Vouvray (France): Chenin Blanc

came a road map for countless consumers navigating aisles of largely unfamiliar products in search of the right bottle to bring home or, perhaps especially, to give to someone else. Scores of 90 or more give a sense of reassurance to those who had been raised in school systems that likewise measured student achievement out of 100. Buying a 90-point wine can give you the same warm fuzzies as earning an A; a 95-pointer, an A+. Incidentally, the lowest possible score in Parker's system isn't 0, it's 50, an insult he applied to 1973 Château Léoville Poyferré. I don't know about you, but I would be morbidly curious to try it.

While humans have spent about forty years obsessing over wine "scores," expecting the drink served at dinner to be graded like so many essay papers, this was preceded by an interlude of some six millennia during which there was appreciation and plenty of connoisseurship, to be sure, but no scale that made claims to be based on such finely calibrated judgment.

I also don't believe in the infallibility of the 100-point scale. No one can say, sans bullshit, that there is an objective difference (other than potential sales figures) between the 94-point Wine X and the 96-point Wine Y. The scale is too precise; it allows too little room for error, human and otherwise.

I'm not alone in this skepticism. Google around and you'll see that other people also doubt whether most critics would make the same judgment of the same wines time after time. Critics of the 100-point system note the variation in human physiology—we all have different numbers of taste buds, for example, and different underlying sense memories that color our experience of what we're sipping. Nor is it likely that wine itself is consistent enough from bottle to bottle to justify the fine grain of the Parker scale, especially at the tail end of the shipping chain, after it's been trucked and handled by God knows who and stored at lord knows what temperatures.

Certain wine people are well attuned to any whiff of criticism about wine criticism itself, and I have received hate mail for suggesting that wine reviewing is less than a perfect science. Let me be perfectly clear, then, that I'm not denigrating wine connoisseurship. Somebody has to keep track of all the nearly countless wines out there and evaluate them, especially the wines that represent a serious investment. This is valuable work and it must be done by someone who has tried enough wines to pick out the true winners. I depend on this work myself.

When an experienced wine critic gives a bottle a 96, I don't believe it's necessarily "better" than a 94, whatever that even means, but it's sensible to give a high-scoring wine the benefit of the doubt. You can approach it with a certain degree of confidence, because a person who tries a lot of wine for a living wanted to signal to us that this particular example is something special in his or her eyes. So if it fits the budget, it can't hurt to bring it home and see if you find it enjoyable, too.

Eventually, however, you may find the confidence to disagree with the experts. The more wine you drink, the more you'll have a firm grip on what you like. I had a pricey Brunello about a week before writing this, a 92-pointer, and I found it too fruity for my taste. I much preferred another wine from the same shopping trip that cost half as much, a Toscana IGT (a less prestigious designation) that the same critic gave an 88.

Here's another way to think of it: You don't need to know a wine's score to determine how well it will do at the dinner table any more than a high score at the Westminster Kennel Club Dog Show determines whether a particular pooch is fun to play catch with. But a prize-winning dog is probably a good dog, and you may as well bring it home to see if you're compatible. Same goes with wine.

SERVING TEMPERATURES

Recommendations for the ideal serving temperature for red wine range from a toasty peak of 68°F/20°C—"room temperature"—all the way down to 55°F/13°C, which, unless you live in a cave or an Antarctic research center, is likely to be somewhat cooler than your abode.

I personally believe room temperature is unappealing. Wine feels thick and sticky when it's too warm. A cellar-like coolness maintains a certain liveliness and vibrancy. What to do? Do you have a big refrigerating device in your kitchen? Splendid. Put a bottle in it about ninety minutes before you plan to drink it. Consider refrigerating your wine for two or three hours if you're later going to decant and rest it on the counter.

As for white, most experts say that refrigerator temperature is too cold, the reason being that you can taste things better when they're warmer, and cold numbs the tongue. It's probably true that a cool, cellar-like 50°F/10°C is worth trying to achieve for a very expensive bottle of, say, Chablis. But for everyday white wine drinking, good old fridge temperature is fine.

TANNINS AND WHEN TO DECANT

You'll read a lot about tannins in reviews of wines, especially reds, because their presence (or absence) is important: It tells you a lot about the experience of drinking a particular wine and whether you will need to decant it before serving. Tannins are naturally occurring chemical compounds (the folks down in the lab call them "proanthocyanidins") that end up in wine mostly through their presence in grape skins and pips (seeds). Oak has tannins as well, and aging for long periods in a barrel can also make a wine tannic. Tannins have no odor, but they create a puckering sensation on the tongue.

Red wines are where tannins are present in high enough concentrations, and certain grapes are higher in tannins than others. Especially tannic are the grape varietals Cabernet Sauvignon, Nebbiolo, Syrah, Tempranillo, and Montepulciano. Wines made from these grapes will tend to age especially well; years locked up in a bottle causes the tannins in a wine to mellow and chemically break down, like a veil that dissolves and reveals a masterpiece.

Lower-tannin red grapes include Primitivo (aka Zinfandel), Grenache (aka Garnacha), Pinot Noir, Barbera, and Merlot. To my mind a lot of terrific affordable wines come from these grapes. They're ready to drink young, and young wine tends to be cheaper than old.

When you are dealing with a tannic wine, decanting—pouring the wine into a neutral vessel to give it some exposure to the air—helps a lot. People sometimes recommend you decant a wine as long as two or three hours, though I think one hour will usually do. If you're like me and you want your wines cool as well as decanted, you'll want to put them in the fridge the day before—or morning of—serving time to get them good and cold. If the temperature and serving time are not quite perfect when dinner's ready, well, neither is life. Coping with that fact is what wine is *for*.

AND NOW FOR THE WINES
Crisp Whites to Drink with Seafood

There are some who truly loathe Sauvignon Blanc, while others maintain that the wines of this noble grape suit any dish you'd be tempted to squeeze lemon on—meaning, I suppose, fish, Middle Eastern cuisine, anything with pesto, even some Thai recipes. Sauvignon Blanc is versatile, and while they're not as cheap as some of the other wines we'll see in this chapter, you don't have to dig too deep into your pockets to buy a nice one from France or New Zealand or even California.

If you're looking for a refreshing, bone-dry white for fish and

TANNINS HIGH AND LOW

LOW: All right to uncork and just drink, convenient for all sorts of occasions

Beaujolais/Gamay Noir

Pinot Noir

Chianti (if not Chianti classico or riserva)

Grenache/Garnacha

Barbera

Merlot

Primitivo/Zinfandel

HIGH: Decant before serving, never drink without food, not ideal to sip at parties

Cabernet Sauvignon

Nebbiolo (Barolo or Barbaresco)

Shiraz/Syrah

Malbec

you don't want to spend a ton of money, you could also try Aligoté. It's from Burgundy, France, and while it stands in the shadows of its more illustrious neighbors made from the Pinot Noir and Chardonnay grapes, Aligoté (which is also planted in eastern Europe and Ontario, Canada) is an overlooked gem.

In the next chapter we'll explore some higher-end options from France for a seafood-heavy dinner.

GRÜNER VELTLINER: ANOTHER SPRITZY WHITE CHOICE

Grüner Veltliner is the wine of the future. Always has been, maybe always will be. A crisp, stone-fruit-scented, minerally white that principally comes from Austria, Grüner is often priced enticingly low because it isn't too well known. Ah, poor Grüner, left standing in the shadow of its Teutonic cousin, Riesling. Grüner is a win-win wine for drinkers: Usually inexpensive but likely to win the approval of any wine geeks in your crowd. They'll think you're buying it because you're in the know about hip, obscure varietals. Ha, ha. Sure, whatever.

PINOT GRIGIO AND OTHER VERSATILE ITALIAN WHITES

When it comes to drinking great wine for a bargain, Italian whites tend to be terrific choices for the tightfisted. I've pretty much taken to buying Italian whites at random, and I've yet to be truly tripped up by the tactic.

Well, there's one piece of advice to follow: As the wine writer Ian D'agata memorably said, Italians do a lot of foolish things but drinking their country's Chardonnay is not one of them. Go for native grapes. Example: Pinot Grigio, which can come out a lot of different ways but typically offers complexity and refreshing zip, to be had for a song. If Pinot Grigio is too acidic for your palate, how about gentler, undemanding Orvieto? Even wines made from the humble, sometimes maligned grape Trebbiano tend to leave me pretty satisfied: They're cheap and simple and don't have a lot of interesting things to say, but they'll be a sunny companion at dinner.

RIESLING

Riesling is a cheerful wine, and my favorite examples shine with aromas of fruit (peaches, pears, apple), followed up by a crisp acidity. It's a wonderful white for a heavy or fatty dish that calls for white wine, such as chicken pot pie or salmon, or anything deep-fried. I usually drink Riesling at Thanksgiving, the traditional North American feast of ~~disgusting excess~~ prosperity and gratitude. It brings enough luxurious complexity for a feast, but it's refreshing, a fact for which you will be grateful as you stuff the last bits of the meal into your mouth.

In Riesling's German homeland, the classification system consists of some downright perplexing terminology. If you want a dry one, you're looking for Kabinett. Other fine Rieslings are made in the Finger Lakes area of New York State, and in Ontario, Canada, but these are difficult to find outside their respective countries.

Incidentally, if you spot a reference to "Hock" or "Moselle" in an old book, these are just antiquated English bastardizations of German regional terms. The wine in question was usually (but not always) Riesling.

ROSÉ MAKES A TERRIFIC GO-TO IN WARM SEASONS AND CLIMATES

About a decade ago someone gave me a bottle of rosé as a host gift, and it seemed like an odd thing to do: I mean, who on Earth drinks rosé? Well, that was then and this is now. Once widely derided as a lightweight, almost silly, wine for girls, rosé is enjoying a resurgence. As I write, consumers are in the midst of a major rethink of pink. The volume of rosé exported from France has more than tripled in our century, with the United States at the receiving end of much of the flow. If this popularity leads to a rise in the price of rosé in its spiritual homeland of Provence, France, perhaps the locals will have to stop drinking it with breakfast, as is their habit. *Rosé* can denote a lovely range of colors: pale orangey-salmon to a deep pink, verging on magenta. Regardless of hue, it's dangerously charming and drinkable when made well. Good rosé tastes wonderful with summery Mediterranean food—especially if it's salty and/or fishy and/or dripping with olive oil—or on its own. Just chill the wine, pop the cork, and chill yourself.

In France, Bandol and Tavel are just two of the well-known rosé appellations. Sweet, sunny Château d'Acquéria Tavel and drier, minerally Château de Lancyre Pic Saint-Loup are good places to start sampling French rosés. They both work as aperitifs.

Spain, Portugal, and Italy make some fine examples as well (I adore the complexity of Faustino V Tempranillo Rosado, from Spain), as do many producers in the New World.

A number of articles have observed that men, especially young American men, are getting into rosé, which has led to the humorous but also obnoxious term "brosé." Remember my rule: There is no such thing as a girl drink or a boy drink. Rosé isn't pink because it's for ladies, it's pink because it's wine that is made using red grapes, but with the skin removed from contact with the juice before fermentation, leaving the wine with a blush color. Anyone who uses the word *brosé* or who makes a stupid joke when a man orders it should be sentenced to drinking tinny house red, really warm, on a hot patio day.

Beaujolais Nouveau/Gamay Noir

Fruity, zippy, and approachably light of body and tannin, Beaujolais is cheap as hell and hits the marketplace when it's just weeks old instead of months or years as, with most other wines. The release of Beaujolais in November used to be a bit of a phenomenon in the 1970s and 1980s, I gather, but wine snobbery has all but crushed the gamine little Gamay Noir since then. Shame. Beaujolais is light on its feet, a red with Peter Pan syndrome. Personally I like lighter reds—they go well with nibbles or with nothing—and they're a boon to cheapskates.

CHIANTI AND OTHER CHEAPER ITALIAN REDS

Italy doesn't seem to produce a lot of terrible wine. Bottles that cost less than the olive oil you're using for the same meal can score well with critics and taste delicious to pretty much anyone. You may have heard that Italians drink wine every day. And how do they afford it? Not by dropping $30 a pop on Barolo.

Among reds, cheap-yet-smooth Chiantis, lithe and leathery, nicely provision a weekday Italian *festa* of pasta or pizza.

You really need to spring for Brunellos, Barolos, and other

WHAT OAK DOES TO WINE

As with whisky, oak will give wine flavors of vanilla (because the compound vanillin is found in oak, the same chemical that gives vanilla pods their aroma) and smoke (because the barrels are charred on the inside). Whereas barrels were once simply the most economical storage method around, winemakers nowadays use oak to give dimension to certain varieties of wine, notably Bordeaux, Shiraz, Chardonnay, and Rioja. How long the wine sits in the barrel determines the extent of these effects, as does the origin of the oak (American or French), the extent of the char, and other factors. When a wine is unoaked, it is usually aged in steel tanks or, in the case of some Italian and other wines, concrete or clay vats (which are as neutral as steel, just less modern). The flavor of an unoaked wine is a more direct transmission of the character of the grape, often brighter and in some sense more "pure."

pricier Italian reds only with steak or for special occasions (see the next chapter). Whereas these wines are nuanced and sophisticated, sometimes you just need to assign a wine to the simple task of washing down dinner, and a big, bold, and not-too-intellectual bottle of Primitivo, Montepulciano d'Abruzzo, or Nero d'Avola is really the best thing for the job.

Robust and spicy but gentle on the tannins, Primitivo isn't exclusive to Italy: When grown and produced in California, it's known as Zinfandel. Same grape (or so say certain DNA tests), different continent.

As for Nero d'Avola, some examples are better than others, naturally, but this big, juicy, charming-but-simple-minded wine seldom disappoints.

If you enjoy Barolo but would like to save a few units of currency, another Piedmontese red to try is Barbaresco. Like Barolo, Barbaresco is made using the Nebbiolo grape and often needs to be at least five years old to be drinkable (the tannins and acidity are formidable in both cases). If giving as a gift or bringing to a dinner party, gently suggest decanting—don't just hand it over without instructions to a relative wine novice. But when you pick a winner, and serve it properly, Barbaresco is a jackpot. If you can buy Enrico Serafino where you live, drop this book and buy a bottle right now. Pair with something meaty and Italian.

WINES FOR TAPAS

How did it take everyone who isn't Spanish so long to discover and adopt tapas, those exquisite, delicious Iberian dishes? Sometime around the year 2005, the rest of the world realized that it didn't have to just stand back and admire the Spanish practice of consuming tiny, salty morsels of goodness during the predinner period. We could play copycat. The persistence of tapas and Spanish cuisine everywhere from London to Oklahoma City since then suggests to me that it's here to stay. We're going to need wine to wash down all those olives and ibérico ham.

Among reds, there are plenty of inexpensive Garnachas and Monastrells to be found. Look to the Yecla region for bargains. Castillo de Monseran is a godsend, a dangerously drinkable and versatile red that balances fruit, caramel, herbs, and some chocolate at a you've-got-to-be-kidding (and you-don't-have-to-tell-the-guests) price. As with Chianti, it's cheap and fun to try a bunch of Yecla reds to see what you like.

You might be tempted to reach for Rioja, a big name in Spanish reds. (And a name that's fun to say. Ree-O-ha.) Go for it, and I'll suggest a lower-priced Rioja Crianza for easy-peasy tapas times. A Reserva or Gran Reserva Rioja is aged longer in oak and is priced higher.

For fishier and light-but-salty tapas plates—of which there are many—you'll want a white wine. Consider sherry: the maritime freshness of a slate-dry fino or manzanilla matches perfectly with seafood and salt. Another bright white possibility: wines made from the Verdejo grape in the Rueda region. These wines offer stone fruit (for example, peach) and pear, minerals, and a bit of juicy zip. Try them with salads or anything with raw or cold seafood—ceviche comes to mind, and don't be too scared to try more unusual stuff like octopus, of which the Spanish are so fond.

Wines for Special Occasions

The perfect wine is a dream that never comes true!

—PIERO ANTINORI, TUSCAN WINEMAKER

TO CHOOSE A GREAT WINE, TRUST THE EXPERTS (AT FIRST)

One afternoon at the newspaper office, an email popped into my inbox from an editor from higher up the totem pole. He was taking some out-of-town bigwigs to a nicely chosen Italian restaurant—critically praised enough to be safe, but noisy and youthful enough to be hip—and, somewhat sheepishly, he asked me to scope out the wine list in advance and make a choice for him that would also come off as savvy.

"Why not just ask the sommelier?" I asked (referring to the term for a restaurant's wine specialist). I told the senior editor that I was familiar with some of the wines but by no means all. Some of them were special-order products where

we live, not available at an ordinary shop. I've been a drinks col-
umnist for a decade, but for most of that time there was someone
else who wrote about wine while I handled all the other drinks. I
wouldn't consider myself a wine expert.

Moreover, there's so much to know that I don't feel as if I
even ought to know it. A sommelier knows her own list. I wondered why this editor wouldn't just ask her for advice.

"Because that's not impressive," the editor said when he came
over to my desk to talk about it.

"But humility is wisdom, and wisdom is impressive," I replied,
which made the editor frown. "Besides, if you try to bluff you can
get really tripped up. What if the list changes between now and
then?"

I did not manage to persuade this editor, but here's hoping I
manage to convince you: All things being equal, it's the experts—
sommeliers, wine sellers, and wine critics—to whom we ought to
turn when we need a bottle for a special night. Draw on their experience. There's even a book about how to fake your way through
a wine list, which leads me to wonder: Why would you ever fake
it? Why not just ask questions and be honest about what you
know and what you need help with?

So that you know at least something, here are a few of the
big-ticket, big-night-out wines you will encounter.

BORDEAUX

Fact number one about Bordeaux is that it's expensive; fact number two is it's ubiquitous anyway. It's the blue-chip choice for a big
red wine; the "rich man's Coca-Cola." France's flagship red wine—
and indeed the flagship of red wine itself—is almost a cliché choice
for that big, meaty, consequential meal, and restaurants tend to
include it on their lists even if their cuisine has nothing at all to do
with France.

Red Bordeaux—known in Britain as claret—refers to a range of styles from the Bordeaux region that can include up to five grapes, Cabernet Sauvignon and Merlot being the dominant ones. Wines from the left bank of the Gironde River tend to showcase big, tannic Cabernet, while those from the right are built around softer Merlot, and on the whole they tend to be less prestigious. (However, Château Cheval Blanc, from Saint-Émilion on the right bank, is quite famous for various reasons, including the yarn about the house guard dog that attacked wine critic Robert Parker while the owner allegedly stood by and watched. Also, unlike most of its neighbors, it's actually made with a majority of Cabernet Franc grapes, not Merlot.)

Whether from the right bank or the left, Bordeaux has a centuries-long reputation for excellence, and the prices to match. Google what it costs in your country to taste a wine from the Premier Cru, or "first growth," wineries, namely Château Margaux, Château Latour, Château Haut-Brion, Château Lafite-Rothschild, Château Mouton Rothschild. Madness, right? Do you even earn that much in a day? In a week? Aren't you curious what these wines actually taste like?

I can't answer for you, but the descriptions are full of words like *rich*, *earthy*, and *smoky*; people discuss the "power" and comment on the leather, as if it were a German car.

Like the passion for a Mercedes sedan, or a Gucci suit, or a Rolex watch, an enthusiasm for expensive Bordeaux can come off as douchey, for lack of a fitter word. Compounding the possibility that you're growing discouraged at this point, let's note that Bordeaux just isn't too trendy at the moment, especially among millennial sommeliers.

Despite all this, we should still be open to the Bordeaux experience. For starters, wine reviewers will happily highlight available Bordeaux that are reasonably priced—some costing a minuscule fraction of the big names—that can give us a hint of the alluring, perfect wines that grace the tables of the rich and famous. (Noted Bordeaux fans whom you may not dislike out of hand reportedly include Tori Amos and Neil deGrasse Tyson.)

For another, the big houses often make so-called second wines—a means of selling off batches that don't quite qualify for the main label. For example, Latour makes Les Forts de Latour, which, despite the second-rate designation, enjoys the approval of wine critics whose judgment I trust.

Overall, when it comes to Bordeaux, if you have enough patience and money, you might figure it all out someday. It seems like a challenge that comes near the end of the wine journey, not the beginning. I'm especially willing to try it if someone else is choosing—and paying.

In the meantime, as a mere mortal looking for a bold, sophisticated wine for a big, meaty dinner, I'm inclined to opt for a Barolo or maybe a Brunello, or a California Cabernet or an Aussie Shiraz. Sometimes it's best to leave the nectar of the gods to the people who carry Olympian wallets.

PINOT NOIR/RED BURGUNDY

Red Burgundy—the French name, which is what you'll see on the label, is Bourgogne—is wine made from the Pinot Noir grape in the region of Burgundy. It has been admired for centuries as a sublime wine experience, the gentle and subtle yin to Bordeaux's bold yang.

Burgundy is smooth and sexy; aromas frequently encountered include cherries, berries, and violets. Examples outside Europe will tend to be fleshier and fruitier, while Pinots from the breezy, blustery Burgundian homeland make stern demands on our ability to sense fleeting aromas and flavors. We sniff at a glass of translucent garnet for passing shadows of strawberry, white pepper, cedar, or cola—even mushrooms, game, and barnyard. As no less a personage than Rush frontman and bassist Geddy Lee told the wine writer Mark Oldman, "I find great red Burgundy to be the most hedonistic, most ethereal, and most graceful of all wine experiences and as a result the most memorable."

At this point it's also obligatory to mention that the Pinot Noir grape is notoriously delicate and requires special care from the winemaker while demanding close attention from the drinker. This was why it was the favored grape of Paul Giamatti's character in the 2004 film *Sideways*—he's sensitive, just like his favorite wine; get it?

Not all Burgundy is priced beyond the reach of the weekday budget: Wine critics regularly identify red Burgundies that offer surprisingly good value by the standards of French wine, despite all the romance attached to the name. You're not going to score anything too affordable from little indie wineries, but there are bargains thanks to the well-known négociants—middlemen, essentially, who assemble the wine and market Burgundy to the world. (I'm grossly oversimplifying their important role; the proof of their value is in the product.) Burgundies from Albert Bichot, Bouchard Père & Fils, Louis Jadot, and Louis Latour have performed admirably at my dinner table, and can help us develop our taste for the princely Pinots that await at higher price brackets.

If you do explore those, the general sense (though I gather there are exceptions aplenty) is that red Burgundies from the Côte de Nuits subregion are known for being beefier than the softer cousins from Côte de Beaune.

A shopping tip: For Burgundy as a whole, 2009 and 2010 were pretty good years, though some other recent vintages were stinkers.

What to eat with Pinot Noir? Try classic French dishes like coq au vin and boeuf bourguignon, escargots, and anything with truffles. Salmon can work, too.

California Reds and Whites

In true American style, the wines of California are known for being big—"hedonistic flavor bombs," in the words of Robert Parker, their best-known champion. They can be redolent of ripe fruit and oak, jammed with flavor compared to their subtler European cousins. I'm not necessarily a fan of California wines, although I've been seduced here and there. Among reds, the blockbuster wines are made from Cabernet Sauvignon and Merlot (as well as blends with these grapes and others, sometimes called "Meritage"—rhymes with *heritage*); the more approachable wines, in my view, are made from Pinot Noir. The famous California white is the Chardonnay, which can be dripping with aromas of gooseberry, tropical fruit, and butter, and because they're heavily oaked, vanilla, too. Even as a skeptic, I can't find anything that goes better with flavorful pork dishes.

You'll really want to carefully consult the reviews to find the bargains and avoid blowing a wad on a dud wine. Outside the States especially, California wines tend to be pricey. The reviews will also help you identify wines made "in a more Old World style" or "with restraint," which is often code for wines that are more satisfying and balanced than the sometimes regrettable, extreme examples.

Brunello di Montalcino

Tuscany produces plenty of easy-to-love, bargain-priced wines: floral-smooth Chianti, Vino Nobile di Montepulciano, and Toscana IGT, among others. They all shuffle to the side like nervous groomsmen when regal Brunello di Montalcino arrives.

The main question is whether one thinks the prices are worth it—$45 is about average for wines that one ideally ought to cellar for another year or three. And these are wines that don't exactly reach out to give you a warm hug. As wine writer Mark Oldman put it, "Brunello requires patience, food, and serious financing . . . [it's] where Tuscany drops its breezy charisma and gets serious."

I haven't loved every Brunello I've tried—sometimes the flavor recedes too far when a sip is competing with a bite of food—yet I've managed to persuade myself that Brunello's high prices are worth paying for a shot at experiencing the sublime examples. The experts advise cellar aging many Brunellos, drinking them a few years (as many as ten to twenty-five) after purchase. All right, but who has a cellar? Not me. A bottle that's at least five years old is sort of ready to drink, but aim for older. Note that 2010 is shaping up to be a knockout year. If you have some way of storing a 2010 Brunello, buy some and wait five years or so before drinking.

Another posh Sangiovese wine is Vino Nobile de Montepulciano; it's worth exploring as a more affordable alternative.

Barolo

The Italian writer Cesare Pavese wrote, "Barolo is the wine you drink when you want to make love on winter days, but only women understand such things." (Wait, wait. I think I understand. What's not to get?)

And as suggestions go, asking, "Anyone for Barolo?" during a festive dinner is equally unlikely to get shot down.

If Brunello is Italy's equivalent of Burgundy—subtle, clever, slick—Barolo could be thought of as its Bordeaux: sometimes masterful, sometimes just a bit too heavy on approach. I personally appreciate this red from the region of Piedmont, made from the grape Nebbiolo, for its big flavors, if not always for the big prices that go with it.

Barolo can be exotic: Tasting notes include things like leather, truffles, and chocolate in addition to less surprising descriptors like herbs and cherry. People get sentimental over Barolo, comparing it to walking through a pine forest in winter. It's worth trying, at least once, to see if you're into it. As I mentioned in the previous chapter, Barbaresco is comparable and more affordable; a good training wine for would-be Barolo enthusiasts.

FOR SEAFOOD: CHABLIS, SANCERRE, AND POUILLY-FUMÉ

For a fancy, slap-up dinner that includes the fruits of the sea, spring for an austerely dry French wine. These can taste like lemon peel and licking wet rock, in a good way—a beautiful way.

These wines are not cheap and, frankly, taste too unforgivingly acidic to consume on their own—they are strictly for washing down food—but when used to crown a meal, they "feel special." When my girlfriend and I make a nice fishy dinner at home, the person who doesn't cook usually picks up the wine. Our go-to choice is Chablis, or as we call it, "cha-bling."

Drink Bubbly Whenever You Feel like It

Tiny bubbles hang above me
It's a sign that someone loves me

—THE NATIONAL, "TROUBLE WILL FIND ME"

A MURMUR OF SURPRISE rippled through the audience during a television appearance when I suggested pairing dry sparkling wine with an oily and crispy dish of latkes—that's Jewish potato pancakes.

Why the shock? I suppose some poor souls don't realize that sparkling wine—champagne and its more modestly priced relations—are the most versatile, flexibly food-friendly beverages known to humanity, other than water. Champagne pairs well with more dishes than cola, Beaujolais, or Riesling. It's delicious with cake and sushi and steak and, perhaps most surprising, fatty, starchy foods: latkes indeed, as well as fish cakes and creamy risotto and buttered popcorn. For simple and delicious, you could hardly beat Laurent Perrier Brut with duck-fat fries. Hooters restaurants made an inspired decision by putting Dom Périginon and chicken wings together on the menu.

Why, then, do people deny themselves the pleasure of sparkling wine until there's a special occasion to justify it? In most countries, if you buy a bottle of bubbly at lunchtime and carry it back to the office, I can almost guarantee someone is going to say, "What's the special occasion?"

I'm tempted to reply, "Well, it's Tuesday. Tomorrow's garbage day. I guess I'm celebrating garbage day . . . eve?"

You don't need a special occasion to drink bubbly. It is itself the occasion. Crack open a bottle whenever you want, just to lift your mood. Imagine coming home from the usual grind, finishing up the chores, and then popping a cork, letting the foamy fizz slide gently into a flute, and bringing the spray of bubbles near enough to tingle your lips and release their yeasty, cracker-like aroma. Old Dom Pérignon called this "tasting stars," and they will merrily descend from the heavens to rescue your crap days.

YOU DON'T NEED A SPECIAL OCCASION TO DRINK BUBBLY.

Some tips: First, a grown-up adult person should call the stuff champagne only if it comes from the champagne region in France. Observe this rule or risk sounding like a rube. And you'll appreciate it more if you save the luxurious frisson of saying, "Let's have some champagne" for those occasions when you actually are.

Second, the following forms of glassware are all acceptable: thin flutes ("champagne flutes"); small, inward-curved white-wine glasses; and old-fashioned, saucer-shaped champagne coupes.

Third, buy yourself a few champagne stoppers so you can stretch a bottle out a couple of days if need be, rather than feeling like you have to finish it all at once. They're easy to find online.

Fourth, keep sugar cubes, Angostura bitters, and lemons on hand so you can switch things up and make champagne cocktails instead of a simple glass of bubbly when you feel like a change. Here's how to make one: Drop an ordinary sugar cube into a champagne glass (a flute can work, but a coupe is preferable in this case). Soak it with two or three dashes of Angostura bitters. Fill the glass with bubbles. Drop a twist of lemon peel into the glass as a garnish. Done.

TASTING CHAMPAGNE

As with any wine, there are lots of little flutters of flavor to experience in a glass of champagne: zesty citrus, notably, and biscuity-yeasty sweetness; I often think of an arrowroot cookie. But your conscious attention is apt to be hijacked by the bubbles.

Oh, the bubbles.

An ordinary sparkling wine fizzes with wobbly balls of carbon dioxide that pop perceptibly, as in a soft drink. A great one surfs into your mouth with pinpoint bubbles so tiny that it feels like an icy-cold cushion of seafoam coasting over your tongue. You can't quite feel the burst, but you will perceive a tingle. Dom Pérignon certainly passes this test, but it's a vintage champagne—it sports a particular year on the bottle—which means it's pricey.

This is not to say you shouldn't buy it. But whether you're getting started with champagne or just picking up a bottle for an ordinary, non-life-changing celebration, you might peer down-shelf or up-menu for something a little more affordable: namely, a nonvintage (NV) champagne.

These vary in style from house to house (in champagne land it's all about "houses"), from the full-bodied Veuve Clicquot (voov klee-KOH) and Bollinger (bow-lahn-ZHAY) to lighter Moët & Chandon (mow-ETT ay shahn-DAHN) and Lanson (lahn-SAHN). My personal favorites are Taittinger (tay-tahn-ZHAY) and Perrier-Jouët (pair-ee-AY zhoo-ETT), or "PJ," as it's known in my house.

You'll note that while I haven't always included pronunciation pointers in this book, I've made sure to do so for champagne: The last thing you want to do when ordering something that costs a day's wages is cock it up by saying it wrong and getting corrected by some pedant.

Another pointer: Independent, so-called grower champagne is on the rise, a sort of indie rival to the well-known, deeply entrenched brands. Try them if you can get your hands on them.

CAVA, CRÉMANT, AND OTHER BARGAIN OPTIONS

To facilitate a sparkling lifestyle, most people will require an affordable alternative to champagne—something that costs around a quarter as much, say. Decent cava fits the bill. Cava is Spanish sparkling wine made in a similar fashion to champagne. Popular, trusty brands include Codorníu and Segura Viudas. I like to keep a bottle in the fridge chilled, just in case it's needed in an emergency. An emergency like a terrible day at the office.

Meanwhile, back in France, plenty of delicious dry sparkling wine comes from places other than Champagne. It costs less mainly because it lacks the brand-name cachet, yet often tastes damn close enough thanks to copycat methodology. This is crémant, and the bottles are labeled according to region—for example, Crémant de Loire (cray-MAHN duh LWAR) or Crémant de Bourgogne (want to pronounce this one correctly? Learn French. Meanwhile just point.).

Another avenue for affordable bubbly is to explore American offerings of the old champagne houses. Louis Roederer set up shop in California to make Roederer Estate, ditto for Mumm and its Mumm Napa. They both offer I-don't-believe-it's-not-French flavor profiles and terrific value. The price gap between champagne and its California cousins will be especially wide and delicious for American consumers.

Some will ask: What about prosecco? I grant that it's a cheerful, affordable, and deservedly popular sparkling beverage, but I grow tired of its sweetness after a while. Is there a limit to how much cava or crémant you can enjoy? I keep trying, and failing, to find it.

OPENING A BOTTLE OF CHAMPAGNE

Sending a cork flying through the air is not the correct procedure, fun as it may look. This book's illustrator and I played in a band with a guy who messed up an eye for decades doing that. Seriously, multiple surgeries. Unless you've just won a Formula One race or have a mortal enemy nearby to aim the cork at, it's not worth the risk. I know I said drinking is supposed to be fun, but—and I hate to sound like your dad—the fun and games will come to a complete stop if someone gets hit in the eye.

Try this instead: Start by removing the cage. Hold the cork tightly with one hand and the neck of the bottle with the other. (Some counsel covering the cork with a tea towel, which improves your grip.) Twist the bottle until you feel the pressure release. This technique is less dramatic than flying corks, but it actually looks pretty slick when you get the hang of it enough to do it with nonchalance. Pro tip: Try to make a bored face, as if to say, "This is just how I do."

Sherry and Other Wines
You Maybe Didn't
Realize Were Wine

I keep a hotel room in which I do my work—a tiny, mean
room with just a bed, and sometimes, if I can find it, a face
basin. I keep a dictionary, a Bible, a deck of cards and a bottle
of sherry in the room.

—MAYA ANGELOU

WHATEVER YOU THINK SHERRY IS, you're
probably wrong. In her wonderful book *Sherry: A Modern
Guide to the Wine World's Best-Kept Secret*, Talia Baiocchi
writes that her beloved wine is "so misunderstood that one wonders whether it was the victim of an elaborate smear campaign
involving all of the grandmas, everywhere."

A conspiracy of sorts did transpire, one fueled by pseudo-
science. Circa 1880, one J. L. W. Thudichum—the best-named of
all Victorian quacks, in my opinion—claimed, entirely falsely of
course, that the presence of calcium sulfate in sherry made it dangerous. Sales of the exquisite Spanish wine, which had been formidable due to its near-universal popularity, promptly cratered.
And they haven't recovered, though there are encouraging developments of late.

Beautifully complex sherry (and its nearly identical cousin,
Montilla) continued to be produced back in Spain. Outside the
country of origin, however, the grandmas who kept the faith
tended to drink bland, sweet, blended cream sherries. Thus was

spawned another stubborn but incorrect idea: Sherry is treacle-sweet and chiefly suitable for the old and stuffy. Mention sherry in an English-speaking locale and people will indeed talk of grandmas; it's one of the most reliable word-association tricks around. (Also: What's wrong with grandmas anyway?)

The truth: a lot of sherry and montilla is actually bone-chillingly dry. I'll admit I enjoy watching the shock spread across someone's face when they try an austere, lemon-sharp, icy-cold sip of fino for the first time.

It's these dry sherries in particular, many of them returning to English-speaking realms for the first time after a long absence, that have wine lovers, sommeliers, and bartenders going gaga.

Oh yes, there's a sherry renaissance afoot, haven't you heard? It's about time, too: For years, fans of sherry—myself included—beat the drum relentlessly, trying to get people to try it. For the longest time the people did not try it. *Would* not try it. The only sherry most people had ever sipped was likely stale, warm stuff from the sideboard. This was frustrating. As my fellow sherry lover Maya Angelou wrote, probably about something far more serious: "There is no greater agony than bearing an untold story inside you."

You'll likely have sherry offered to you at some point, so you'll want to at least be prepared to accept a glass without frowning and slagging off grandmas.

What is sherry? To repeat, because this point seems to have a lot of trouble getting through for some reason: Sherry is wine. Full stop. Forget about the "fortified" part (most sherries are indeed juiced up with a bit of brandy, which is what *fortified* means, but many of the drier ones aren't). It's actually best to think of sherry and montilla as a family of truly interesting wines that are united by a set of time-honored techniques and a common origin in a hot coastal region of western Spain. When we talk

SHERRY IS WINE. FULL STOP.

about sherry, we're using the English name for Xeres, once spelled Jerez. It's a chalky, breezy part of Andalusia that's reputed to be among the most welcoming, charming, and food-loving areas in the world.

Flavor-wise, sherries are all over the place, but quite handily, there are various terms that can help you navigate.

In an attempt to acquire the taste all at once, you could grab sherries of a few different varieties and try them all with one multi-course meal. Start with the driest and proceed to sweeter ones as the meal progresses. Fino and manzanilla sherries are the tongue-sucking, spine-shivering dry ones, and they're straight-up delicious with olives, fish, and seafood, and salty snacks of all kinds—even salt and vinegar chips (aka crisps), as I have shirtlessly observed on my back patio. The Spaniards use these sherries to wash down summer tapas. Drink them ice cold.

Amontillado sherries are where sherries start to shift from dry as a sunburn to somewhat easier drinking, and start to have shades of dusk to their color—the best are like the beautiful golden hour between daylight and sundown.

Getting darker and sweeter now, we may be lucky enough to encounter the relatively rare palo cortado sherries, which are a little sweet and complex and are oxidized, meaning they can carry a whiff of bruised apple.

Then we come to dessert-worthy oloroso sherries, which are typically deep and nutty, and work well on their own. Oloroso often works with cheese, as does palo cortado. Incidentally, spent oloroso barrels are much coveted by the scotch industry, which uses them to add spicy, dried fruit (prune-like) flavors to the whisky.

Finally, at the end of the sherry rainbow we have brown-sugary Pedro Ximénez sherries, or "PX" to aficionados, which can be black as crude oil and sweet as a Christmas cake. I think it's one of the great dessert wines, up there with Tuscan vin santo.

SHERRY COCKTAILS

Sherry is experiencing a revival as a wine in its own right, but it's also long been a friend to bartenders. It works better than most other wines in cocktails, probably because the flavors are concentrated enough to hold together when diluted and mixed. Sherry also has interesting textures to offer, including sharp acidity and smooth sweetness, depending on the kind of sherry it is. Try these recipes and see.

Sherry Cobbler

The go-to thirst-quencher for American women in the 1860s, the sherry cobbler is a pretty straightforward union of sherry, sugar, and crushed ice. It was the last ingredient that made it seem fresh and new back in the day—the sherry cobbler is often credited for helping popularize the use of ice in drinks. It's also said that the straw came into common use through the cobbler. So at the very least, we owe the cobbler the honor of being dusted off and revived in the twenty-first century, and bars are doing just that. Bellocq in New Orleans, for example, made it the signature drink of the house.

Bear in mind there is plenty of latitude in regard to the sugar and fruit. You can also make cobblers using port, Madeira, and many other wines, not just sherry.

Basic Cobbler

- 4 ounces sherry
- 1–3 teaspoons powdered sugar (aka icing or confectioner's sugar); amount depends on your taste and the sweetness of the sherry
- 2 thin orange slices
- Any fruit, for garnish

Add crushed ice, sherry, sugar, and orange slices to a cocktail shaker and shake well. Pour everything, ice and orange included, into any glass that works. Add more ice if necessary so that the brim is "cobbled." Arrange the garnish fruit artfully atop the ice. Serve with a straw.

ADONIS

I like to prepare the Adonis in batches as a welcome cocktail for parties. It's a craftily cheap way to fill 'em up with one serving before you've even done any work. To a pitcher, add 2 parts sweet vermouth (Cinzano Rosso would be my choice), 1 part sherry (switch it up later if you like, but start with palo cortado or dry amontillado), 1 dash orange bitters, and 1 ice cube per serving. Stir and leave the mixture in the fridge while you await your guests. Put your feet up and throw a record on. The similar **armor cocktail** is 1 part sherry and 1 part vermouth, with 1 dash orange bitters per serving; procedure as above.

CORONATION COCKTAIL NO. I

The coronation is another batchable cocktail: Mix 1 part dry sherry and 1 part dry vermouth (try Noilly Prat), and add ½ teaspoon maraschino liqueur, 1 ice cube, and 1 healthy dash orange bitters per serving. The procedure is the same as for an adonis. For a **bamboo cocktail** just leave out the maraschino.

PORT

Some readers will feel that I've apportioned space to sherry and port in a rather imbalanced way, perhaps in a manner that reflects the author's own preferences and biases. The reader would be correct: In general I find port too sweet. That doesn't mean you will, too.

Ruby port is the cheap stuff and that will be the place to begin your sampling of Portugal's main contribution to fortified wine. Should you experience a hint of enjoyment here, keep exploring; other, posher categories of port include tawny, colheita, and late-bottled vintage. Chilled white port, meanwhile, makes a fun patio beverage, particularly as an aperitif or dessert wine. The same philosophy applies as with sherry: If you don't dismiss it as an old person's drink, you might discover a wine you never knew you wanted.

As with all fortified wines, port will keep well for a number of weeks after opening, if refrigerated. My port-loving friends reminded me to warn you that a port hangover will crush you flat, so exercise caution.

MADEIRA

Hailing from the island of the same name off the coast of Africa, Madeira is Portugal's other contribution to fortified wine. After suffering an even deeper crash in popularity over the twentieth century than port or sherry did, the Madeira revival lags a few years behind.

Madeira was born as an Atlantic trade good, and today one of its claims to fame is that it is aged in wood at high temperatures—105°F/40°C to 115°F/45°C is typical—and this is meant to simulate a voyage in the hold of a ship rolling in toasty-warm Caribbean waters, or languishing in some sweaty harbor. Madeira's other claim to fame is its incredible longevity: It's the Galapagos tortoise of wines; it can continue to improve after a century in the cellar.

The wine is made from a number of unfamiliar-sounding grapes. Many Madeiras won't tell you which varietal(s) are within—they just say something like "fine old Madeira" and you just have to shrug and plunk your money down for a surprise ride—but if you see the word *Sercial, Verdelho, Boal/Bual,* or *Malvazia* on the label, it refers to the grape involved. I've listed them in order from light and dry to dark and sweet. Rainwater Madeira lies in the middle-dry territory and is mostly found in the United States. It was created for the American market; Washington and pals adored Madeira and got hootered on the stuff to celebrate the Declaration of Independence—and considering they were signing up for a possible date with the hangman, good for them. Anyway, I find rainwater Madeira to be lovely stuff, a pretty little before- or after-dinner wine.

MARSALA

Sicily's answer to fortified wines, Marsala is best known today as a cooking wine—it's used in chicken Marsala, a dish that also involves mushrooms.

I understand that in Sicily, and perhaps in certain well-stocked London wine shops, you can find far better examples of Marsala than the flat-tasting stuff we typically have available most other places. Perhaps the better Marsalas will take off as a hip wine the way sherry has, and as Madeira is fixing to do next. Until then, it remains dormant.

VERMOUTH IS
NOT THE ENEMY

I want a really dry martini. Just put some vermouth in the air
conditioning.

—TYPICALLY HOSTILE TWENTIETH-CENTURY
ATTITUDE TOWARD VERMOUTH FROM A CUSTOMER
AT THE ANCHOR BAR IN BUFFALO, NEW YORK, AS
REPORTED BY JOSEPH SCOTT AND DONALD BAIN IN
THE WORLD'S BEST BARTENDERS' GUIDE, 1998

A T A PARTY, a pretty young woman once asked, while
watching me refill my glass, "Ugh? Who just drinks vermouth on its own?"

"Italians," I replied with my smuggest grin. That worked out
for me about as well as you might guess, but I was right about one
thing: In its twin homelands of France and Italy, vermouth is
thought of as a popular light, bittersweet predinner beverage. The
whole anglophone hesitation over vermouth, including the notion
that it must be mixed with something else before it becomes drinkable, bemuses and puzzles them.

It seems vermouth's sad fate is to be misunderstood in the
wider world. For one thing, most people don't realize it's wine—
"aromatized" wine that started off as the product of some indiffer-
ent grape like Trebbiano. It's wine all the same, wine that has been
given new life with the addition of spices and a kick of brandy, not
to mention sugar.

Vermouth comes in two principal varieties: sweet and dry,
which are referred to as Italian and French, respectively, in older
books—an accurate reflection of their origins. Incidentally, even

sweet red vermouth is made from white wine; added caramel gives it a reddish-brown color. The word *vermouth* is related to *wermut*, German for "wormwood," but as far as I can tell, wormwood is not an important component of modern vermouths. Sweet vermouth is a key ingredient in the Manhattan and the negroni, and dry vermouth is a cornerstone in the martini. Vermouth is called for in many, many other drinks, but its appearance in these three power-houses makes it a must-have for any bar, public or private.

There are also amber and white (bianco) vermouths, but these have never really caught on in English-speaking countries. And this is a shame: A white vermouth like Martini Bianco, chilled and with a little ice and a splash of soda, can be a lovely way to shift the gears of one's mental machinery from "toil" to "play." Hints of orange peel, caramel, and gentian flit into your consciousness and pull it away from whatever it was that seemed so important at three in the afternoon. It's not unusual to see people ordering a glass of vermouth as an after-work beverage in Turin, Milan, and Florence. (See "Aperitifs," on page 223, for more on the predinner drinking rituals of southern Europe.) For TV producer Rita (played by Andie MacDowell) in the film *Groundhog Day*, a vermouth on the rocks with a twist reminds her of Rome. A simple glass of Carpano classico on the rocks with a ribbon of orange peel is a wonderful thing: refreshing but tart. As we will see, the Italians believe it stimulates the appetite. I'll often fix myself a glass to sip while starting up the barbecue, just to make sure that appetite will be there later, when I need it. You can't be too safe.

The big barrier to vermouth appreciation is the fact that peo-ple's typical first (and last) experience is with dead vermouth. What's dead vermouth? That forgotten bottle that was left at the back of the bar, at Grandma's house, wherever. Someone opened the bottle and poured some into a cocktail. Then it was left behind to fester. Eventually the flavor seeped out. When you went to grab the same bottle, presumably also to make a cocktail, you tried some of the vermouth on its own. It was flat and flavorless. Verdict reached.

If you're willing to give vermouth one more chance, make sure you pour yourself a fresh glass. Open a new bottle. Pour a good glug on the rocks. Have an orange at the ready if it's sweet vermouth or a lemon if it's dry or white, but first just try the soft-textured liquid on its own.

What you'll encounter is a sweet little bouquet of flavor, something like ordinary wine but much gentler—certainly less acidic—and at the same time more mysterious thanks to the addition of spices, herbs, and such. As with so many other southern European products, the recipes of vermouth are concealed in a contrived cloak of secrecy.

Speaking of freshness, we're fortunate to live in a time when vermouth is being treated as a new experience. It (and other fortified wines) is something of a trend in non-Mediterranean countries, from Japan to the United States to the Netherlands. Vermouths, including Noilly Prat, Dolin, and Carpano Antica Formula are receiving the praise and reverence they always deserved.

The various brands of vermouth can be quite different from one another. I personally enjoy Carpano Classico, Cocchi Vermouth di Torino, and Guerra (which is Spanish) as my sweet vermouth for most applications. Carpano Antica Formula makes a negroni or Manhattan sing like Pavarotti—during the long, dark years when you couldn't get it Canada, I knew people who took to smuggling it in. When you splash Carpano Antica on the rocks, a bittersweet and slightly medicinal concerto of vanilla, dried fruit, and root beer cries out into the air. Among the lesser sweet vermouths, Cinzano rosso and Dolin rouge will do in a pinch.

For dry vermouth you'll want something French. Go for Noilly Prat if you can scrounge it, and settle for Dolin dry otherwise. For bianco, you might have trouble finding anything but Martini & Rossi but that's all right: It's delicious, especially with a garnish of basil.

HOW TO DRINK SAKE

On a moonlit night, a snowy morning, or beneath the
flowering cherry trees, it increases all the pleasures of the
moment to bring out the sake cups and settle down to talk
serenely together over a drink. . . . And it's a fine thing when
someone who really hates having sake pressed on them is
forced to have just a little.

—YOSHIDA KENKŌ (C. 1283–1350),
BUDDHIST MONK AND AUTHOR, *ESSAYS IN IDLENESS*

MAGINE IT'S YOUR FIRST NIGHT in Tokyo—ever.
You head to the Shinjuku Golden Gai because you read that it's
where Japanese people from many walks of life, from salarymen
to punks, like to unwind at the end of the day. And moreover, this
close warren of tiny bars is perennially threatened with being
knocked down to make way for new construction, so it's wise to
see it while you can. The locals are likely washing the day away
with nama biiru (draft beer) and whiskey mizuwari (whiskey with
ice and cold water), but you're excited to be in Japan so you want
sake, the national drink.

The first thing you'll want to know is that locally they simply
call it nihonshu (日本酒), the literal meaning of which is "Japanese
alcohol." Flipping through the sake menu of a high-end izakaya—
in Japan, it's often a binder with laminated pages of labels, orga-
nized regionally—you'll quickly discover that the world of rice
alcohol is astonishingly vast. You might be presented with a lot of
options, and it's difficult to know what's what. Moreover, the gulf
in quality between good sake and bad is enormous, while the
prices are relatively close together. This is one of those instances
when it pays to invest in getting it right.

So here is the phrase that will bail you out: *"Osusume wa nan desu ka?"* meaning, "What do you recommend?"

That will get you sorted most of the time, but it probably doesn't hurt to give you a little primer so you don't feel totally at a loss. While often referred to as rice wine in English, sake arguably has more in common with beer in terms of how it's made. The carbonation produced through fermentation is generally allowed to escape in the case of sake. (However, you will occasionally spot a sparkling sake. Some of them are artificially carbonated, others naturally.)

Quality sake is best served cold. Warm sake is more traditional, but since the 1980s or so, aficionados have preferred the chilled option to preserve the floral delicacy of the drink. Great sake is light and perfumed with melony and berrylike fruit aromas, which you lose when it's warmed. Still, as Japanese poets and boozehounds have written for hundreds of years, you really can't beat warm sake on a cold night.

Cold sake is the obvious choice when pairing with sushi, but don't just drink sake when consuming raw fish. Other times and places are suitable. Take the bath, for example. Japan is a nation of people who love to soak in hot water. I rediscovered the simple pleasure of taking a bath while I was visiting there, and since returning home I've made a habit of sipping chilled sake while soaking in the suds. Sake just feels right anytime you're immersed in hot water.

Now to decide what to drink. Once again the world of nihonshu is vast and the terminology complicated, and it comes from a language with the world's most brain-straining writing system. I've gone to the trouble of memorizing a few terms that usually lead to solid results.

The first is junmai (純米酒). Most sakes contain at least a small amount of distilled rice alcohol (called jozo) to enhance and preserve flavor. Junmai sakes contain none. A junmai sake is a "pure" sake, from a certain point of view, and may be relatively less fragrant compared to other high-end sakes. It's assertive and raw.

The other terms to remember are ginjo (吟醸酒) and daiginjo (大吟醸酒); pronounce with a hard *g*. Sake is made from rice that has first been polished. The further the outer layers of the rice are milled and polished away and the smaller the little white nub left for brewing, the higher the quality of the sake (at least in theory). These sakes have been polished to an especially high degree; to make a ginjo sake, at least 40 percent of the rice kernel is milled away. To make a daiginjo (it essentially means "big ginjo") the rule is 50 percent, meaning less than half of each grain must be left before the rice can be brewed into sake. Ginjos and daiginjos are especially fragrant and delicate. They are the pinnacle of the sake brewer's craft; you owe it to yourself to try a ginjo and/or daiginjo at least once. They will be relatively inexpensive at a grocery store.

These designations can also be combined if they both apply. For example, a sake that is a junmai daiginjo (純米大吟醸) is probably pretty special.

Another one to try once—and possibly just once—is nigori sake (にごり酒), which, rather than carefully filtered, is just run through a coarse cloth. This leaves it white and milky and relatively sweet. If you like it, and that's a big *if*, you'll probably prefer it at dessert.

Now let's imagine you find yourself among the lesser sakes, much in evidence across Japan's beloved 7-Elevens. Experts advise looking for the term futsushu (普通酒), rather than zojoshu (増醸酒). The latter can be dire. In Japan, low-end sakes come in big, plainly adorned containers that look like milk cartons. It might be fun to get drunk on them and ride around on public transit, but you may end up feeling like hell the next day.

If you care to be a little more refined, you can drink sake out of the little clay cups designed for the purpose. To go even more old-school, the real tradition is to use cedar boxes called *masu*, which you might be able to find in a store specializing in Japanese goods. I think the purists sniff that the cedar ruins the flavor of the sake, but it's great fun to watch the liquid dribble down your friends' chins as they contend with the unfamiliar square shape. Whatever vessels you use, you're supposed to fill them right to the brim. When drinking in Japan, remember that filling one's own glass is considered rude and filling other people's is polite; that *kampai* means "cheers," and that the Tokyo Metro rudely shuts down at the inopportune hour of midnight.

There are other rice-based drinks to be found in China, Korea, and Vietnam and in places where the diasporas from these countries gather. My best advice: Look helpless and someone may take pity and assist you.

PART III

HOW TO CHOOSE, DRINK, AND SERVE COCKTAILS AND SPIRITS

Stocking Your Home Cocktail Bar: The Gear, and How to Use It

So, do you like . . . stuff?

—RALPH WIGGUM (*THE SIMPSONS*)

HERE'S A THOUGHT if you're hesitant about making cocktails: Maybe just go out and buy some of the gear and see if it inspires you. I never smoked ribs or tried snowshoeing before I owned a smoker and snowshoes. Obtaining these items forced me to learn how to use them. Now there's hardly anything I enjoy more than smoking a hunk of meat or treading down a trail of white powder in winter.

It probably also helped that in both these cases I ended up with decent, American-made brands. In the world of cocktail gear, it's often Japan that makes the top-quality stuff, and much of it is beautiful to behold. If you can afford Japanese-made shakers, mixing glasses, bar spoons, and strainers, go for it.

FIRST, YOU MEASURE

Even if you plan to keep your operation pretty bare-bones, you need tools to measure the liquor with. No matter how many times you may have seen a bartender free-pour—and no matter how dweebish this is going to make you feel in comparison—it's preferable to measure. Cocktail making is a precision art. As in baking, the ratios between ingredients are often important, and you can make a mess of things if you start pouring willy-nilly. Many cocktails hit or miss depending on how well balanced they are, and the human eye simply isn't a precision instrument.

Jiggers are the traditional measuring vessels of the cocktail trade, and far better than shot glasses for the purpose. I don't use jiggers too often, but if you want to go that route, you'll want a few different ones to be able to measure commonly used amounts—½ ounce, ¾ ounce, 1 ounce, and 1½ ounces.

Better still, I think, are mini measuring cups. Oxo makes terrific ones with angled measuring lines that let you easily see how much fluid is inside without having to crouch and squintingly take a look from the side view. Depending on what country you buy them in, they might have metric lines on them, which is helpful for cocktail recipes originating in Europe. Finally, common measuring spoons are fine for portioning out small amounts like a ¼ teaspoon or ½ teaspoon.

Here are some measurement equivalents that can be handy to keep in mind (note that if you live in Australia, tablespoons are bigger for some reason: 20 milliliters instead of everyone else's 15 milliliters):

1 teaspoon = 5 milliliters
1½ teaspoons = ¼ ounce
1 tablespoon = 3 teaspoons = ½ ounce = 15 milliliters
20 milliliters = ⅔ ounce
30 milliliters = 1 ounce
2 ounces = ¼ U.S. cup
1 U.S. cup = 8 ounces = 240 milliliters = 16 tablespoons = 48 teaspoons
1 U.S. quart = 4 U.S. cups
1 liter = about 4.2 U.S. cups

(Disclaimer: 30 milliliters doesn't equal exactly 1 fluid ounce. Note that there are two slightly different fluid ounces anyway, the American and the imperial—but it's all close enough for us to be comfortable with this common shorthand. A *certain amount* of imprecision won't ruin your drinks.)

GEAR FOR SHAKING, AND HOW TO USE IT

There are exceptions, but for the most part you prepare cocktails using the shaking method when they contain juice, milk, cream, or any other opaque ingredient.

For shaken cocktails, you'll want, obviously enough, a cocktail shaker. Many households already come equipped with what's called a cobbler shaker. (Who bought it? Why do you have it? Who knows?) They're vase-shaped with a removable lid, and usually an even smaller removable cap that comes off to reveal a built-in strainer. This kind of cocktail shaker is attractive to amateurs because it's relatively easy to use. Professionals, on the other hand, tend to disdain them. A cobbler shaker is difficult to keep clean—bits of gunk always find a recess to cling to in the dishwasher—and the parts have a habit of sticking together at the most inconvenient times.

The more in-the-know option is what's called (for some reason) a Boston shaker, which consists of a large metal tumbler and a glass (or smaller metal tumbler called a "cheater tin") that fits inside (see 1 in the illustration on the next page). A Boston shaker might take a bit of practice to master. But it's like learning to shoot photos using film or learning to drive with a stick shift: Master the hard way first and the rest follows naturally.

Get started by grabbing the mixing glass, which resembles a straight-sided pint glass and sometimes is indeed a 16-ounce U.S. pint glass. The tin stays to the side for now. If the recipe calls for muddling anything, do that first. Then add liquid ingredients as directed (2), followed by ice. How much ice? Lots. There's a school of thought that says you should fill the mixing glass to the very top. It's just frozen water, so why not? Knock yourself out.

Next it's time to affix the tin, which you do by fitting it atop the glass at a slight angle—not straight up and down; but at a slight

1   2   3   4

angle, like the way a tap dancer would wear a fedora—and giving it a firm, downward thump (3). This will create a seal, which you can test by lifting the whole shaker by the tin only. The glass should come with it (4). Suction! All hail physics.

Now you're ready to shake. Keep the glass side toward you, so that if the shaker comes unsealed for whatever reason, the drink will spill on you (ha, ha! funny blooper) and not on your guest/customer (not so funny). Don't just shake up and down. Give it some side-to-side motion as well. Really work it (5). By the way, they say your cocktail-shaking face is also your sex face; something to bear in mind. Shake until the tin feels as cold as it's going to get.

After you've given it about 15 seconds and the cocktail is satisfyingly cold and mixed, it's time to release the seal. Hold the shaker with a firm but gentle grip on both the glass and the tin, at the same time, with one hand—like holding a newborn baby's head up while also supporting the neck. You'll want to hold it with the tin side facing the floor and the glass side pointing at the heavens. Now look at the glass. Because the tin sticks on a bit of a cocked angle, the glass will lean to one side. Think of that side as noon. Using the heel of your hand, deliver a little smack to the side of the tin right about where it makes contact with the glass, at 3 o'clock (or 9 o'clock if you're left-handed) (6). You should find it

5   6   7

becomes unstuck fairly easily. If not, you must be throwing a party or giving a demonstration—problems always seem to happen when everyone is watching. Put a stuck shaker aside, wait, and eventually the seal will weaken enough for you to separate the parts at last.

If/when you have successfully separated the tin from the glass, the cocktail and ice will be in the tin, waiting for you to strain. The standard kind to use with a shaken drink is called a Hawthorne strainer, and you'll recognize it by the horseshoe-shaped coil along the bottom.

Fix the strainer to the top of the tin and pour the drink out through it into the glass. The strainer traps the ice. This is what a cocktail recipe means when it says "strain" (7). Practice before you perform in front of others. Bartender Jeffrey Morgenthaler recommends getting used to shaking by using rice. You'll be able to hear it moving around in the shaker, and it's easier to clean up than a liquid if you spill it everywhere. Sounds like a plan.

Finally, if you'd prefer to work with somewhat less room for error (that is, without the possibility of broken glass), plenty of bartenders have taken to replacing the mixing glass in a Boston shaker with a squat metal "cheater tin." Otherwise, the technique is the same.

GEAR FOR STIRRING, AND HOW TO USE IT

Cocktails that principally consist of alcoholic ingredients—meaning some combination of spirits, wines, and bitters, but no juice, cream, or carbonated ingredients—are usually stirred, not shaken. Stirred cocktails may also contain sugar in some form. Occasionally a recipe that includes a modest amount of lemon juice will be stirred rather than shaken for the sake of ease.

When a cocktail recipe calls for stirring, begin as you do with a shaken recipe. Start by getting any muddling out of the way, then add the booze, then the ice—two-thirds of the way to the top of the glass. And stir. Not like you would stir soup, but by sticking a long spoon down into the ice and swirling it around in a circular motion. Keep trying; you'll get the hang of it. Do it gently enough that the liquid does not spill out the sides of your mixing glass. This can be a calming, meditative experience.

Stir until the drink is ice cold. This might take a minute—I mean a literal minute, as in sixty seconds. Condensation will start to coat the outside of the glass when you're approaching the right temperature, and the aromas wafting through the air will begin to reach your nostrils (I usually figure the drink is ready when I can smell it).

You can stir cocktails in the glass side of your Boston shaker—when a recipe calls for a "mixing glass," it can refer to this. But it looks a hell of a lot slicker to have a distinct mixing glass for martinis and Manhattans and their boozy kin. Rare in our time is the cocktail den that doesn't sport a tidy line of yarai (diamond-cut pattern) mixing glasses from Japan, with thick sides and a built-in spout. They make for worthy possessions: elegant looking but sturdy. Whatever mixing glass you use will likely be big enough to make two cocktails at a time, or more if you spring for an especially large one.

Stirred cocktails usually call for a different kind of strainer, a perforated number called a julep strainer, though ownership of one of these is optional if you already have the Hawthorne kind. They really just do the same thing.

A long spoon, one with a corkscrew twist along the shaft, is also required for stirring. Japanese barspoons sport different butt ends for performing different tasks. The ones with a fork on the end, for example, are for spearing cherries. The rounded and blunt ends are for muddling soft items: A blunt-ended barspoon is terrific for smooshing the sugar cube in an old fashioned, something to keep in mind if you're a fan of those.

Notwithstanding all of the above, never let a lack of equipment hold you back. If you don't have a mixing glass or barspoon on hand, you can use a large glass (a pint glass, perhaps?) and a chopstick for stirring. In desperate situations or hard times, a saucer can act as a strainer.

Other Bar Tools

Citrus squeezers come in different sizes, for limes, lemons, oranges, and even grapefruits. Because quality cocktails are always made using freshly squeezed juice, you'll want to have this useful tool.

Vegetable peeler, for removing the peel from citrus fruits. There's a huge gulf in quality between the default version from the supermarket and a nice vegetable peeler from a kitchen supply store. Go with Swiss or Japanese made, if available. A **citrus peeler** is a different kind of implement; you can use it to make long, thin twists but otherwise it plays less of a role in cocktail making than vegetable peelers do.

A **muddler** is optional, and particularly recommended if you enjoy mojitos. It's a small bat (as in a stick, not the flying mammal) that you use to squish ingredients at the bottom of a mixing glass, gently or violently as di-

BACK ROW, LEFT TO RIGHT: Oxo mini measuring cup, jigger.
FRONT ROW, LEFT TO RIGHT: vegetable peeler, Hawthorne strainer, julep strainer, three barspoons, muddler, lime squeezer.

rected. It's often used for herbs and fruit, but you can also use a muddler to flatten the sugar cube in an old fashioned. There was a time, around 2005, when the cocktail world was in the grips of muddle mania, but that has abated for now. You'll still want to have a muddler on hand to press the mint in a mojito.

ICE: MORE IMPORTANT THAN YOU MIGHT REALIZE

Why do fancy cocktail bars use such big ice cubes? Because it melts slower, thanks to a smaller surface-to-volume ratio. Or so the story goes; drinks writer Kevin Liu did some experimenting and found that the effect is not as significant as the craft cocktail movement assumes. Anyway: Big, two-inch ice cube molds are easy to find these days, and especially useful for devotees of the old fashioned.

You also need tools to make itty-bitty crushed ice out of normal-size domestic refrigerator ice. In cocktail land it's usually the strong summery drinks that contain crushed ice: the mint julep, the zombie, some versions of the daiquiri. All contain a generous glug of hard spirit if made properly. If they pack too much kick on that first sip, crushed ice will melt within a few minutes and, thanks to our friend dilution, you're off to the races. Moreover, as the ice melts, your beverage stays cold.

To smash ice, don't use a blender. A wooden hammer called a schmallet works far better (I'm not authorized to share the story behind that name but it's a bit of an inside thing anyway). You pair it with a Lewis bag, which is a canvas sack originally designed for transporting coins. Cocktail gear specialists usually sell a mallet and Lewis bag as a set. Fill the bag with ice and, as Homer Simpson would say, bash it good.

HOW TO GARNISH

There are two kinds of maraschino cherries. The original kind are almost black in color and come from Italy or Slovenia. They are delicious. Luxardo is the principal brand of real cherries. The bright red kind sold in English-speaking countries are an inferior knock-off. The difference is immense, and so is the cost. Cheap cherries, which I call "clown noses," are a false economy.

A certain quotient of personal flair and creativity can go into your garnishes, but before you engage in any Pinterest-fueled flights of fancy, practice making a basic citrus twist—the thumb-size strip of peel that appears in the modern version of the old fashioned and countless other drinks.

Use your high-quality vegetable peeler to take a small amount of peel off the lemon or orange. You're interested in the waxy, colored part; avoid the layer of white pith underneath, which tastes bitter. Trim the peel with a knife to make it look pretty if you like. Squeeze the lemon peel to spray the essential oils onto the surface of the drink. Rub the peel on the rim of the glass, then attach it as a decoration. Serve.

GLASSWARE

Finally, you'll need glasses to put all your drinks in. Five kinds are essential.

Heads up: When a bartender or recipe (or this book) mentions a "cocktail glass," it means something specific: a stemmed glass with a relatively small capacity. The ideal cocktail glasses fit about 5 ounces of liquid.

Especially in vogue are rounded ones that are also referred to as "coupes." Coupes were originally used as champagne glasses (though nowadays sparkling wine enthusiasts prefer tall flutes or even white-wine glasses, which keep the carbonation healthy longer). There's a common cocktail party story about coupes being based on the shape of Marie Antoinette's breasts. It's not true.

The glassware company Libbey's "Embassy" champagne glasses are sturdy and affordable. Also, cocktail supply stores and vintage shops (and even flea markets) often have vintage cocktail glasses sporting unique shapes and lovely etching. These are better places to shop for cocktail glasses than big-box housewares stores,

BACK ROW, LEFT TO RIGHT: highball, Collins, margarita
(also called a coupette)
FRONT ROW, LEFT TO RIGHT: two shapes of cocktail glasses, rocks
(also called an old fashioned glass)

which sell ones that are far too big—8 ounces or larger. A martini looks ridiculous in a glass that huge.

Speaking of martinis, the conical-shaped "martini" glasses of the mid-twentieth century, which are just a particular shape of cocktail glass, are currently desperately out of fashion.

Rocks glasses are squat tumblers that hold your drinks on the (wait for it) rocks. They're also called old fashioned glasses, after the most popular cocktail served in them. A good size is 8 ounces; double old fashioned glasses are also available, with a capacity more in the 14-ounce range, but I don't own any and have never lamented their absence.

Margaritas get their own special glass, which you'll need only if you make margaritas. Once again, vintage finds have a more reasonable capacity (5 ounces or so) than newly bought ones, which can be obscenely large.

Highball and Collins glasses are both tall and skinny and hold iced drinks. Classic highballs (8 to 12 ounces) are shorter and somewhat wider than taller, skinnier Collins glasses (10 to 14 ounces), but their size ranges overlap. For simplicity's sake you may prefer to keep a small fleet of 12-ounce glasses that will work in recipes calling for either a highball or a Collins.

Stocking Your Home Cocktail Bar: The Liquor and Assorted Other Things

Perfection is achieved not when there is nothing more to add,
but when there is nothing left to take away.

—ANTOINE DE SAINT-EXUPÉRY

'M OFTEN ASKED: What should I buy if I want to have a home bar? The answer isn't too complicated. You can get by with ten or twenty bottles of backbone spirits, and the rest of the ingredients—sugar, fortified wines, mixers, and so forth—will come and go as you need them. And needless to say, it's more important to know how to use what you actually have than to stock your bar in a certain way.

I may advocate the elegance of simplicity, but I personally find that advice tough to follow. A home bar can easily get out of hand under the stewardship of a crazed liquor hoarder. Ahem. My own minimalist spirits lineup, if I could ever stick to it, would be built like so:

- Start with a good, junipery London dry gin, because that's the most essential spirit of them all for cocktails. Beefeater, Boodles, and Broker's are terrific all-arounders.
- White rum, because you can't make a daiquiri or mojito without it. Brugal, Bacardi, and Havana Club all make nice, affordable ones.

- A relatively dark, slightly posh rum (say, Mount Gay Eclipse, The Scarlet Ibis, or Appleton Estate Reserve), the kind of rum you can pour into a snifter and drink neat.
- Both bourbon and rye whiskey (the latter can be from the United States or Canada); for a cocktail whiskey the 45 percent ABV mark is about right.
- A good but inexpensive 100 percent agave tequila (El Jimador will work)—opt for just a reposado if you want to stick to one bottle, but if you're an especially big agave fiend, keep on hand one blanco and one reposado, and consider a mezcal as well (Del Maguey Vida will ⸴ work fine).
- Cognac (overproof Pierre Ferrand is ideal for cocktails if you can get it; Rémy Martin VSOP works well otherwise).
- Vodka, if that's your thing or your friends' thing (I don't particularly care which vodka, but the Polish ones tend to be nicer than average).
- Cointreau.
- Campari.
- Angostura bitters.

And while you tend not to use Irish whiskey or Scotch in cocktails too often, it's a good idea to keep one of each around for people who simply prefer a dram to a mixed drink. You probably won't offend anyone worth your trouble if your choices are Bushmills Black Bush and The Famous Grouse; they're widely appreciated and generally respected—and pretty affordable, which you'll appreciate if you entertain.

That's around fifteen bottles. Are we done? Not quite yet. You still need a few things for the pantry and fridge. You can't go very far in cocktail fixing without sweet and dry vermouth. You'll want fizzy mixers, too: ginger ale, cola, tonic water, and club soda. Buy cans in bulk and put out only as many as you need on each occasion.

Keeping stocked with all of the above makes for a good start on the classics of cocktail making. Depending on what drinks you plan to make that day, you will need to have a freshly replenished bowl of oranges, lemons, and/or limes. Perhaps mint or grapefruit, too. Obviously, pick up anything else you happen to need for a particular recipe.

SECOND-TIER INGREDIENTS

Contemporary cocktails call on a greater liquid repertoire than was considered reasonable a century ago. If you're scanning magazines for recipes from our own time, or trying to mimic what they do at your favorite swanky cocktail joint, you'll soon discover the drinks of the twenty-first century require certain things that the classics usually don't. Mezcal, challenging though it may be, appears often. Peychaud's bitters won't go to waste. You might need genever here and there.

Meanwhile, absinthe and sherry appeared often in the drinks of a hundred years ago, disappeared for a number of decades, and have resurged to become important ingredients again. It's not a bad idea to have these on hand as well if you're combing the Web for up-to-date drinks. For a generic cocktail sherry, look for a medium-bodied one—for example, one that says "amontillado" on the label.

As for liqueurs beyond the basic orange ones, you'll buy those on a case-by-case basis, as you need them. See "Essential Liqueurs," on page 90, for a hint of which ones are called for most often. Be judicious. They pile up.

Essential Liqueurs (and Some Nonessential Ones)

Ahh. Sweet liquor eases the pain.

—TROY MCCLURE (*THE SIMPSONS*)

MUCH AS IT MAY BE DIFFICULT for a bartender in the English-speaking world to believe, liqueurs were not actually invented to be mixed into cocktails. They were conceived as after-dinner cordials, sweetened with sugar. Some people may still consume them this way, but you and I are more likely to know liqueurs as sweeteners and flavoring agents for cocktails.

Which ones should the would-be home bartender keep at home? Here are a few, roughly in order from most to least essential. For the minimalists out there, you could accomplish plenty by just having Cointreau and maraschino.

ORANGE LIQUEURS

You can't travel too deeply into the cocktail canon without some orange liqueurs from France. Completists and enthusiasts will want to have Cointreau, Bénédictine, and Grand Marnier, in that order of priority.

Cointreau is the plainest and most versatile orange liqueur, made with a neutral base (that is, a flavorless alcohol, akin to

vodka). Incidentally, if you're using an old cocktail book and you spot the word *Curaçao*, you're all right to use Cointreau instead of the orange liqueur from the island of Curaçao.

Your home bar will go through a lot of Cointreau. You may be tempted to go with a generic brand, but don't. I advocate being a cheap bastard where appropriate, but money by substituting generic triple sec for Cointreau is not a case where cheapness is rewarded.

Pierre Ferrand Dry Curaçao does, however, make a classy alternative to Cointreau. This relatively new product, which has cognac as its base, enjoys the cocktail connoisseur nod of approval but it is quite dry indeed (they do warn us right there in the name).

If you swap it in for Cointreau, be ready to add a bit of simple syrup to rebalance things.

Pricey-but-worth-it Grand Marnier is also made with cognac instead of a neutral alcohol base, and it has a more autumnal, rounded, warming flavor as a result. Some recipes for margaritas and sidecars call for Cointreau but I usually prefer the sweeter effect of Grand Marnier. The basic version of Grand Marnier is tasty enough, but the higher-end varieties are delicious sipped from a snifter after dinner. That's how Grand Marnier is consumed in French-speaking regions.

Bénédictine is a French orange liqueur with a brandy base, and with spices and roots added to the mix. You use Bénédictine in a number of vintage cocktails, including the vieux carré (see below), Bobby Burns, and brainstorm (see page 178), and see page 211 for the dead-simple formula for a Bénédictine and brandy, or B&B.

Vieux Carré

This cocktail's name means "old square." Le Vieux Carré is what New Orleans's French Quarter is called in French. Without the sweet, herbal orange of Bénédictine to smooth it out, a vieux carré would be too harsh to drink. As it is, the cocktail is as gentle as the slow rotation of the Carousel Bar at the Hotel Monteleone, which is where you should have one.

- 1 ounce rye whiskey
- 1 ounce cognac
- 1 ounce sweet vermouth
- 1 teaspoon Bénédictine
- 2 dashes Peychaud's bitters
- 2 dashes Angostura bitters
- Twist of lemon peel, for garnish

Add the rye, cognac, vermouth, Bénédictine, and both bitters to a mixing glass with ice. Stir until the mixture is very cold. Strain into a rocks glass with ice. Garnish with a twist of lemon peel.

CRÈME DE CACAO

Crème (rhymes with *them*) de cacao (kuh-COW) is simply chocolate liqueur, and would probably sell better if they just called it that. It pops up in quite a lot of vintage recipes (the twentieth-century cocktail being my favorite) but not many contemporary ones. I suspect that's mainly because culinarily minded bartenders aren't overly pleased with the mass-produced crèmes de cacao on the market, which are too sweet and don't offer the same complexity that quality chocolate does.

Craft distilled alternatives are starting to appear, mercifully. For example, Tempus Fugit's crème de cacao, with a hint of vanilla, tastes like a posh boutique chocolate bonbon—but best of luck finding it.

Whatever you're able to get your hands on, crème de cacao is essential in a brandy Alexander—although if you live in Canada, try Criollo salted caramel liqueur for a tasty alternative.

Brandy Alexander

It tastes like a milkshake, you can down one in a few seconds, and there are a couple of ounces of liquor in there. What could go wrong? Everything. As the Feist and Ron Sexsmith tune "Brandy Alexander" warns us, this is an old-time drink that "goes down easy" and is apt to get you into trouble. I like to drink these around the holidays, when getting slightly more drunk than planned is slightly more culturally sanctioned than usual.

- 1 ounce cognac
- 1 ounce light (18%) cream
- 1 ounce crème de cacao (or Criollo salted caramel liqueur)
- Freshly grated nutmeg or quality dark chocolate, for garnish

Add the cognac, cream, and crème de cacao to a shaker with ice, shake well, and strain into a deceptively dainty little glass. Grate a little nutmeg or dark chocolate on top and take it nice and slow.

MARASCHINO LIQUEUR

This is your bar's secret weapon: an ingredient that few among the general population are consciously familiar with, but which lends cocktails and punches an irresistible touch of fragrant sweetness.

Maraschino (pronounced mair-uh-SKEE-no, not SHEE) is made in northeast Italy and Croatia by infusing alcohol with the pits of cherries—not the flesh. It doesn't taste like cherries. It tastes like . . . heaven. It's a pleasantly nutty, aromatic, and sweet flavor that I'm afraid I'm unable to describe too well despite years of trying. Just buy a bottle and see for yourself.

Luxardo is by far the dominant brand of maraschino liqueur, recognizable by its straw-covered green bottle with a red cap and white label. I once called the bottle ugly in my newspaper column and someone from Luxardo wrote back sounding very hurt. (But it *is* kind of ugly.)

Among many other cocktails, you'll find maraschino in the martinez, which is (maybe? probably?) an ancestor of the martini. Not everyone is convinced about its lineage but appreciation of the flavor is nearly universal: It is like a martini, but sweeter—more cheerful, somehow. I prefer a martinez to a martini four days out of five.

Martinez Cocktail

- 1½ ounces gin
- ¾ ounce dry vermouth (preferably Noilly Prat)
- ¼ ounce sweet vermouth
- ½ teaspoon maraschino liqueur
- 2 dashes orange bitters
- 1 quarter-size piece of lemon peel, for garnish

Add the gin, both vermouths, the maraschino, bitters, and ice to a mixing glass and stir for at least 30 seconds. Strain into a chilled stemmed cocktail glass. Squeeze the lemon peel to spray the essential oils onto the surface of the drink and then float it on the surface.

CHERRY BRANDY

This is the one that does taste like cherry. The Danish brand Cherry Heering is the gold standard here, and while it's included in a wide variety of relatively obscure vintage cocktails, you're going to end up using most of it in Singapore slings, a truly fine hot-weather refresher. Here's the correct recipe; ignore all other versions like the meaningless static they are.

Singapore Sling

- 1 ounce dry gin
- 1 ounce cherry brandy
- 1 ounce freshly squeezed lime juice
- 1 ounce Bénédictine
- 3 dashes Angostura bitters
- Soda water
- Maraschino cherries, for garnish

Fill a Collins glass with ice and add the gin, cherry brandy, lime juice, Bénédictine, and bitters. Stir. Top with soda water and garnish with cherries. **Tip:** You can stir with a chopstick, then thread cherries onto it.

ST-GERMAIN

If you're not British, French, or Scandinavian you might not be familiar with the scent of elderflower and elderberry. If you are from those places, where these flavors are an integral part of the diet, their lychee-like sweetness is likely well nestled in the warmest, deepest parts of your olfactory cortex.

Either way it's an appealing scent. St-Germain, a French-made liqueur, was so popular during the first decade of the twenty-first century, appearing in so many cocktail recipes, that the liqueur was derided as "bartender's ketchup." If you make a lot of modern-day cocktails, you'll want to have this in the house. The massive, heavy bottle would also make a fine murder weapon. Colonel Mustard, in the library, with the elderflower liqueur.

Some Other Liqueurs to Consider Keeping Around

- Crème de cassis, if you like to transition to the evening with a kir or kir royale
- Drambuie, if you like a rusty nail
- Crème de menthe, if you enjoy stingers
- Sloe gin, if you're partial to drinks from the 1920s or 1970s. And make it real sloe gin, like Plymouth or Hayman's—many cheapo brands don't actually contain gin
- Amaretto, if you're a sucker for an amaretto sour
- Blackberry liqueur, if you enjoy a bramble, which is an English cocktail that also contains gin and lemon juice

A SHORT AND SWEET
BRIEFING ON BITTERS

If I ever feel a cocktail is flat or missing something, the answer
is almost always bitters.

—BARTENDER JAMIE BOUDREAU

A DMIT IT: If a cough medicine doesn't taste too bad,
you'll take an extra little sip, won't you? Any medicine
that's tasty enough eventually turns into a recreational
beverage. That's where cocktail bitters come from.

In the first category of bitters are aperitifs and digestifs. These
tend to be European and are drinkable by themselves. We look at
these types of bitters in part 4.

Right now we're talking about the more concentrated style of
bitters that flourished in the Americas from the eighteenth through
the twentieth century. While they're still used as aids to digestion—
a few dashes of bitters with soda or ginger beer
settles many a Trinidadian stomach—to most of
the world, these have evolved in purpose to become cocktail ingredients almost exclusively. Bitters are to cocktails as herbs and spices are to
cooking. In the simplest terms, they're mixtures of
flavorings preserved in alcohol or a glycerin solution. They often feature roots, herbs, and spices,
resulting in a medicinal flavor, but sometimes the tincture is made
to capture sunnier aromas like fruits and flowers. Although cocktail bitters are often (but not always) alcohol based, like vanilla

> BITTERS ARE TO
> COCKTAILS AS
> HERBS AND
> SPICES ARE TO
> COOKING.

extract they're sold in grocery stores because they're flavoring agents you use a few drops at a time; they're not something you would ever drink enough of to get intoxicated. They're considered a food product, in other words. Bitters tend to come in small bottles because a little goes a long way.

To add bitters to a drink, give the bottle a firm downward shake so that a few drops shoot out. That's a dash, as called for in many cocktail recipes. Just a dash or two makes all the difference in drinks from the old fashioned (which is some two centuries old) to cocktails being dreamt up as we speak.

Which bitters should the home cocktailer keep around? In my experience only a few are called for on a regular basis. I present them in descending order of usefulness.

ANGOSTURA BITTERS

Around 1820, an intrepid German doctor named Johann Gottlieb Benjamin Siegert left Europe for Venezuela, where he became the chief surgeon in Simón Bolívar's revolutionary army. By the time he left Bolívar's service four years later, Siegert had perfected a proprietary brand of bitters that, like a twenty-first-century superfood, played on its exotic South American origins to sell abroad. The bitters didn't even contain the bark of the angostura tree; the name just sounded cool.

The formula for Angostura bitters is a secret (this is typical) but seems to include heavy amounts of clove and a European mountain herb called gentian. You can't make an old fashioned or a Manhattan without Angostura bitters. Ditto for dozens of lesser-known vintage recipes. People are still inventing uses for Angostura bitters. All of this makes Angostura the most essential brand to keep around. You have to have a bottle if you're going to have a home bar, it's that simple.

Incidentally, no one quite remembers why the label is always too big for the bottle (there's an official story about confusion between two brothers, but it's too cute to believe). Anyway, that's the tradition and they're sticking with it.

ORANGE BITTERS

As the name suggests, orange bitters are, well, orange. Specifically, orange bitters contain the essential oils contained in the peel, which gives them a fresh, zesty quality. The most versatile, all-around handy brand is Regans' No. 6. You'll need orange bitters to make classic cocktails such as the bijou and Bronx, not to mention an orthodox pre-Prohibition martini. It's wise to have them on your bar.

PEYCHAUD'S BITTERS

Distinguished by their aggressively red color, Peychaud's bitters are, like Angostura, a mix of various herbs and roots and so on. They're not as bitter as Angostura and give off earthy flavors and a hint of anise. Try them the way booze geeks test bitters: Drop a little on the back of your hand and then sniff at it, and finally lick your hand clean. You'll see this ritual everywhere should you ever visit the annual Tales of the Cocktail event in New Orleans. That's where Peychaud's are from, by the way: They're named for Antoine Amédée Peychaud, a nineteenth-century French Quarter apothecary. Peychaud's bitters are called for in classic New Orleans cocktails, principally the sazerac and vieux carré, and contemporary bartenders continue to invent cocktails calling for a drop or two of the deep red. If you're serious about cocktails, it's worth investing in a bottle.

OTHER BITTERS

Peach and celery bitters are occasionally helpful, followed by Amargo Chuncho (useful in pisco sours) and chocolate bitters.

But for the love of God, don't buy any of them until you're actually sure you're going to use them. Bitters pile up. A bottle may look tiny, but if you expect to go through six dashes a year at most, even a single bottle can be a lifetime supply. You'll never get rid of them. You'll have bottles all over the house. Your choice is between minimalism and accumulation, in other words. In the latter instance you'll end up with a collection to bequeath to your grandchildren—a bitter legacy, as it were.

SOME ADVICE ON
SERVING COCKTAILS

Cocktails have always appealed to me because they
involve mixtures, experiments, paraphernalia, testing,
tasting, finally serving.

—KINGSLEY AMIS

HOW TO READ A
COCKTAIL RECIPE

Having covered the essential weights and measures and the basic
techniques of stirring and shaking earlier, you should find cocktail
recipes fairly straightforward. Just follow the procedure, *don't employ any shortcuts or dodgy substitutions*, and your drink should turn
out fine. It's not magic; bartenders just make it look that way for
tips.

You'll do much better if you're also equipped with some essential lingo, like so . . .

You produce a dash of bitters by taking the cap off and giving
the bottle a good downward shake into the drink, as if you were
trying to dislodge ketchup that won't flow. What comes out counts
as one dash, bearing in mind that a fuller bottle makes for slightly
bigger dashes.

A chilled glass means just that. I put it in the freezer for a few
minutes. Pro bartenders fill it with ice for a minute or two, then
empty it and fill it with the cocktail. My way is easier.

To double strain, you pour the drink through second strainer—

a fine mesh strainer—while also using a cocktail strainer in order to clarify a drink somewhat. For example, a double-strained side-car or margarita contains less citrus pulp than an ordinary one. I don't often bother double straining, to be honest.

Unless otherwise noted, *ice* means cubed ice.

Old-timey recipes sometimes use ratios rather than measured amounts. They typically assume that one cocktail contains about 3 ounces of liquid ingredients, so, for example, if the recipe says "half gin, half vermouth," use 1½ ounces of each. Also, if a vintage recipe calls for Curaçao or orange Curaçao, use what we now call triple sec—or Cointreau, to name the standard quality brand.

For simple syrup, read on.

HOW TO MAKE SIMPLE SYRUP

Many cocktails call for a premade liquid sugar called simple syrup. The name don't lie; simple it is. Prepare it in large batches and it will keep in a food container for a few weeks—somewhat longer if you tip in some vodka as a crude preservative.

To make it, mix equal parts sugar and water (say, 1 cup each) in a saucepan and heat gently—do not boil—while stirring until the sugar is all dissolved. This takes a couple of minutes. Sometimes "rich" simple syrup, or 2:1 syrup, is called for, in which case you use twice as much sugar as water. If you encounter the term *gomme syrup* or *gum syrup* in an old cocktail recipe, 2:1 simple syrup will do just fine. To make gomme syrup you're supposed to dissolve some gum arabic in the simple syrup to make it silky; I've done this, and it's lovely. But in our hectic world, who has the time?

HOW NOT TO SCREW UP
YOUR COCKTAIL PARTY

Your first cocktail party will be a mess. Sticky counters, dirty glasses everywhere, cocked-up cocktails poured down the drain. It's okay, this happens to everyone, and you'll get better. Be sure to make your mistakes around people who won't mind so much. I find siblings and one's oldest friends make for splendid guinea pigs.

Here are some tips on how not to foul it up too badly. If it sounds as if I did these things wrong before I did them right, that is, of course, the case.

First, keep your cocktail party small. Start with four guests plus yourself. If you're new at making cocktails, you won't be able to cope with more than that. Eight people is a maximum, even for the experienced. It's going to be hectic in your kitchen or at your home bar, which of course is not set up with anything like the same efficiency as a real bar.

Second, make a "welcome drink" that you can prepare ahead of time and serve to guests as they arrive. With stirred drinks, you can make a big pitcher at once and stick it in the fridge to keep it cold. Something weak works great for this (see the recipes on pages 62–64 that use sherry).

Third, you weren't thinking of actually giving your guests a choice, were you? No, no, dear me, don't. No. Make cocktails in rounds and don't let anyone stray from the program. "Who's up for a Manhattan? Show of hands," and so on. I used to fuss around with making menus and such. Cute, but behaving like a real bar complicates matters exponentially.

Fourth, never get high on your own supply. I'm afraid when you're hosting, it's beer for you, friend—*at most*. If you're not strict about this, you can fall into a "one for you, one for me" routine, serving yourself an example of everything you make. You won't have any memory of your guests departing for the evening, because you'll have been passed out on the couch while your partner apologizes.

Fifth, amass your ice with the enthusiasm of an Old Testament king hoarding piles of riches. For a four-hour cocktail party, every guest will hoover up about half of a 6-pound bag of ice, so buy three or more bags and fill all your trays to be safe. When the ice runs out, so does the fun. (Even as I write this I'm fairly sure most of you will ignore my ice advice the first time around. For some reason everyone seems determined to learn this lesson the hard way.)

Sixth, at a certain point you will have hit your limit of mixological usefulness, unable or unwilling to make another cocktail, no matter how easy. This will coincide, of course, with your guests' epiphany to the effect that all they want to do from now on is drink cocktails. Congratulations, you've made converts. Now to distract them. Have a cold bottle or two of bubbly ready to offer them as a diversion, so that you can finally sit down and enjoy a drink of your own.

GIN AND HOW TO DRINK IT

The gin and tonic has saved more Englishmen's lives, and minds, than all the doctors in the Empire.

—WINSTON CHURCHILL

PRIMORDIAL FORMS OF GIN first bubbled to life in the laboratories of medieval alchemists, and spirits of juniper have been transmogrifying into countless forms and guises ever since. At different points along the way, gin has been thought of as a medicine (a cure for PMS and flatulence, among other complaints), a harsh but effective consolation for the desperate underclass, an everyday punch ingredient, an everyday cocktail ingredient, and a spirit suitable for women and men alike. Gin has been considered quintessentially Dutch, quintessentially New York, quintessentially Raj, quintessentially English.

Today gin may be considered indispensable from the point of view of booze connoisseurs, but in most countries it steadily lost popularity over the twentieth century. Its current trendy rediscovery—what a long way it has traveled since its days as a fart encourager!—has not restored gin to the daily lives of the masses. I suspect gin is written about more than it is actually consumed.

Gin is a paradox: It exhibits a distinct, unmistakable pine resin and spice aroma thanks to its distinguishing ingredient, namely, the berrylike cones of the juniper bush. Yet despite its aromatic assertiveness, gin can almost hide when mixed with other ingredients in cocktails. The shapeshifter of the speedwell is most closely associated with the martini and the gin and tonic, both sophisticated, dry refreshers that must be served ice cold. Yet there are hot drinks built around gin, and it mixes with flavors you wouldn't think would work at all. Take tomato, for example; gin functions surprisingly well as a substitute for vodka in a bloody Mary. Many are the miracles of this trickster god.

Meanwhile, the flavor can pose quite the challenge to the uninitiated. Everyone balks the first time they bring gin's oily-sweet, coniferous vapors within olfactory range, especially if for some reason they're trying it neat. (No one's asking you to do that, by the way, so don't. The few people I know who consume gin straight are pretty hardcore enthusiasts.)

My initial, youthful sip of gin convinced me that adults had simply confused it with floor cleaner. I didn't touch it again for years. If you're similarly discouraged, I would say keep trying. Gin is among the most important tastes to acquire for those who would be complete drinkers. But enough of my peer pressure. Let's proceed to practicalities.

WHAT IS GIN?

People sometimes get confused and think gin is distilled out of juniper, but that's not quite right: Gin is a neutral spirit (effectively just vodka—and, like vodka, typically made from grain), that is flavored with "botanicals," either through an extra round of distillation or in a cheaper process known as cold compounding. These botanicals are a potpourri of roots, herbs, fruits, spices, and sometimes flowers. Distillers have a lot of latitude when choosing them, and different brands' characteristic flavor profiles differ quite a bit from one another.

A gin may contain as few as four botanicals, as is the case with the original Tanqueray (namely, juniper, coriander, licorice, and angelica root). In some of the newer-fangled craft gins, the botanical counts run into the dozens. (Gimmick? You decide.)

Aromatic coriander seed, orris root (a flavor fixative), and perfumey angelica root seem near universal, and many gins make use of citrus peel as well. The one botanical that must always be included, by definition, is juniper. Used for millennia as a folk medicine, the dark purple orbs look like berries and have the texture of berries, but they're a trick of nature: not berries at all, but fleshy cones in a berry disguise. Track some down—at a specialty herb shop, for example—and nibble on them. You'll discover juniper "berries" are not just hot and resinous, but also sweet, a trait that is more discernible in some gins than others.

Gin is a cosmopolitan spirit; its ingredients are gathered from around the world. Commercial juniper nowadays comes principally from Italy and Bulgaria, coriander often comes from Morocco, and other botanicals that meet in the same bottle can be sourced from parts as distant from each other as Canada and Indonesia.

A great portion of the gin maker's art isn't so much the recipe as the skill at sourcing the botanicals. Consistency can be tricky to pull off. Once when I visited the Beefeater distillery—a former pickle factory in the slightly rough-around-the-edges London neighborhood of Vauxhall—master distiller Desmond Payne was in the midst of choosing coriander seed batches for the year. His worktable had around twenty little numbered dishes on it, each containing a different sample of Moroccan coriander. He held them up for me to sniff. Some were fresh and fragrant, others savory and almost tomato-like. Making gin is complicated.

TYPES OF GIN

When people say *gin*, they almost always mean London dry gin. (As I do when I use the word *gin* elsewhere in this book.) Close your eyes and think of three gin brands, if you can. Perhaps Gordon's, Tanqueray, and Gilbey's? Or do you think of newer, posher brands, like Martin Miller's, Aviation, and Sipsmith? Well, they're all London dry gins.

This oily-dry, crisp style of gin is the kind most people have encountered since about 1880. I like my London drys assertive, barking like a British drill sergeant and spitting on my face with a hot breath of oily juniper. A slug of Beefeater or Broker's or Boodles, none of this pussycat Bombay Sapphire business (that stuff is barely gin, by the way; it was developed in the 1980s as a softer, less junipery gin for the uninitiated, and it shows).

I've heard it suggested that some of the contemporary craft-distilled gins on the market, the ones with less traditional flavor profiles, constitute a distinct new category of gin—something different from the London drys of yore. They often contain botanicals that were unheard of until recently. Greenhook Ginsmiths, of Brooklyn, calls its beautifully floral gin "American dry." And can you really call Hendrick's a London dry gin? That's difficult to say. Its flavors of rosewater and cucumber are prominent and unusual. They smell terrific, and a martini made with Hendrick's is a fresh-tasting delight (I garnish these with a thin slice of cucumber). The trouble is that you can't just use a weird contemporary gin like Hendrick's willy-nilly in vintage recipes. For starters, it wouldn't go too well with cream, I should think.

To help you explore different gin brands, I've divided some common, worthwhile London dry(ish) gins into four categories on the basis of price and whether they have an old-school juniper-and-spice composition or if they're more contemporary and exotic.

A mention does imply a recommendation: I enjoy all of these gins immensely and imagine many others would feel the same.

Beyond London dry, we're into much rarer forms of gin. Genever is the Dutch form of gin; it's older and indeed the original on which the English styles were based. It's so different from Lon-

SOME GIN BRANDS

LOW-COST, TRADITIONAL (USE IN VINTAGE COCKTAILS)	HIGH-COST, TRADITIONAL (USE IN VINTAGE COCKTAILS)
Broker's	Martin Miller's
Tanqueray	Junípero
Hayman's	Victoria
Beefeater	Sipsmith
Boodles	Hayman's 1850 Reserve
	The Botanist
	Whitley Neill
LOW- TO MID-COST, MODERN (MAY NOT WORK IN EVERY RECIPE)	**HIGH-COST, MODERN (MAY NOT WORK IN EVERY RECIPE)**
Magellan	Hendrick's
Bulldog	Blue Ribbon
	Greenhook Ginsmiths
	G'Vine Floraison

don dry that some people insist we shouldn't really use the English word "gin" for it at all. That's an argument for the diehard booze geeks.

Genever is made from malted grain and is less aggressively junipered than London dry, which means it's sweeter and much better suited to drinking neat. In the Netherlands and Flanders it's used as a beer chaser called a *kopstoot* (head butt); in Amsterdam I was shown how you're supposed to fill the glass to the very brim and bend down to drink it like a horse at a trough rather than lift the vessel and risk spilling the precious liquor. (Well, either that's the tradition or the Dutch are playing a brilliant, elaborate joke on visitors.)

Outside the Netherlands and Flanders, you're more likely to find genever in cocktails. It makes a nice old fashioned. Drinking it this way was big in New York in the nineteenth century. You'll find plenty of genever cocktail recipes out there, some from that era and more from our own time.

In between genever and London dry you have Old Tom, a sweeter, rounder, archaic form of English gin. It was the gin Dickens would have known. Gin-slinging London bars in his day would hang a wooden tomcat outside as a form of signage for the illiterate, to advertise its presence of gin within, hence the name. While this cat mostly died out during the early twentieth century, it has found a new life in recent years thanks to distillers including Anchor (of California), Ransom (Oregon), and Hayman's (England). Most of them have a cat somewhere on the label. Cute. The recipe section of this chapter includes a couple of uses for Old Tom. Obscure though it may seem, it's handy to keep around for cocktails old (Tom Collins, martinez) and new.

Our final category is Plymouth gin. It's similar to London dry gin, and there's only one brand of it: Plymouth gin, formerly Coates Plymouth gin. While it's true that Coates & Co. of the western English city of Plymouth won some sort of court case to gain recognition for the local style of gin, it's more of a sibling to London dry than a cousin: sweeter than the norm, but with a distinct family resemblance. Beyond the semantics, Plymouth gin makes for a killer martini. I enjoyed Plymouth gin a lot more before they dramatically and suddenly hiked the price a few years ago—in some countries, it now costs far too much to keep around the house on a regular basis. Shame.

THE GIN AND TONIC

Everyone should know how to make a gin and tonic: They're popular, and suitable for many moods and seasons. Properly made, a gin and tonic is clear and effervescent in appearance but with a baroque botanical fugue to the senses of smell and taste. It's a dark symphony full of diminished chords, from quinine and grapefruit sharps to juniper and coriander flats.

Thanks to the bittersweet bite, it's refreshing but not so yielding and easy drinking that you're tempted to down it all in one shot. The gin and tonic tastes like something the Italians might have invented, and I certainly mean that as a compliment.

Actually, maybe we shouldn't credit the British: They say necessity is the mother of invention, and that's certainly true of the gin and tonic. The British came up with tonic water as a delivery system for the antimalarial drug quinine, which it still contains, despite the relative unlikelihood of contracting malaria on your back patio. Its debut, circa 1860, coincided not only with the United Kingdom's growing imperial thirst but also with the rising acceptance of once-scandalous gin among the British upper classes. So while gin and tonic probably originated in some squalid barracks in India, it rapidly climbed to the potted-palms-and-linen-tablecloth environs of the private club.

How to make a solid tonic? Start with a ratio of 2 parts tonic to 1 part gin and adjust from there, restrict the ice to two or three cubes, and add a squeeze of lime.

For the tonic, my favorite is Fentimans. Coming from England, it's a fancy-pants craft tonic (don't laugh; they're a thing) and a lovely choice if you like bitterness. Among the more plebeian, easily found options, the orangey, firmly quinine-infused Canada Dry works for me over Schweppes any day.

OTHER GIN COCKTAILS

Tom Collins

The once-mighty, largely forgotten Collins originated in mid-nineteenth-century London as a single-serving punch. The other way to look at a Collins: You're simply making yourself sparkling lemonade and gin. Either way, it's a refreshing, basic drink to keep in the tool kit.

- 1½ ounces Old Tom or London dry gin
- Juice of ½ lemon
- Club soda
- 1 teaspoon superfine or quick-dissolving sugar
- Lemon or orange slice and cherry, for garnish (optional)

Add the gin and lemon juice to a 12- to 14-ounce Collins glass. Fill the glass with ice and stir. Top up the glass with soda, then (the exciting part) sprinkle the sugar on the surface and stir again to generate tiny bubbles. If (and only if) you're entertaining, go to the trouble of garnishing with a citrus slice and/or cherry. If you enjoy a traditional Tom Collins made with gin, try white rum (which makes a **Ron Collins**), tequila (a **Juan Collins**), or genever (a **John Collins**) next time.

Pegu Club

In 2005, Audrey Saunders opened a retro cocktail bar in Manhattan and dubbed it the Pegu Club, after both the cocktail and the gentlemen's club the drink was named after, which had stood in Rangoon (now Yangon). Saunders's bar played a major part in the revival of the vintage cocktail in New York, and its influence was felt around the world. This is my version of a Pegu Club cocktail. You can add sugar or reduce the lime juice as your palate dictates.

- 1½ ounces gin
- ½ ounce Cointreau or Grand Marnier
- ¾ ounce freshly squeezed lime juice
- 1 dash Angostura bitters
- 1 dash orange bitters
- Lime wheel, for garnish

Add the gin, Cointreau, lime juice, both bitters, and a big handful of ice cubes to a cocktail shaker. Shake well and strain into a chilled cocktail glass. Garnish with the lime wheel.

Hanky Panky

- 1½ ounces gin (try something assertive, like Beefeater or Plymouth)
- 1½ ounces sweet vermouth
- 2 dashes (say, ½ teaspoon) Fernet-Branca (or other very bitter amaro)
- Twist of orange peel

Add the gin, vermouth, Fernet-Branca, and ice to a mixing glass. Stir until the mixture is ice cold and then strain into a chilled cocktail glass. Squeeze the orange peel to spray the essential oils onto the surface of the drink. Use the peel as a garnish.

THREE MORE TERRIFIC VINTAGE GIN-AND-JUICE COCKTAILS

The last word cocktail is one of those weird-but-it-works cocktails from the opening decades of the twentieth century. It hails from the still-exclusive Detroit Athletic Club. It starts refreshing, with gin and lime juice, but the plot thickens with the addition of mysterious maraschino liqueur, and the final note is of Chartreuse (a French liqueur covered in "Digestifs," on page 232), which gives the cocktail a finish like a cold question mark.

That the last word would emerge from a chilly city is no surprise; the cocktail makes a terrific response to any debate about whether you can have a gin drink in winter. Every sweet-tart sip is an icily confident yes. There's a whole family of recipes that combine gin with citrus juice and one or more extra ingredients that add sweetness and interest, all of them swirling with enough flavor for a snowstormy night. The twentieth century, for example, softens the gin with Lillet (an aperitif wine), lemon juice, and crème de cacao. Lemon, chocolate, and juniper? Yep. Somehow it works. The aviation is gin, lemon, maraschino, and crème de violette (a purple liqueur flavored with violets), or sub in the equally purple Crème Yvette if that's all you can get your hands on. Other family members of this cocktail family include the corpse reviver no. 2, the casino, and the white lady.

Last Word

Unbelievably, this deliciously complex drink was forgotten for decades after Prohibition. Even the Detroit Athletic Club lost track of it, according to the Detroit Free Press's *Sylvia Rector. It was only a mention in an obscure 1951 cocktail book that prompted Seattle bartender Murray Stenson to rediscover the drink in the 2000s, and from there it reconquered the world. Actually, forget the "re" part; there's little evidence it conquered anything the first time around. And thus can a round of last words work as a fitting toast to second chances.*

- 1½ ounces gin
- ½ ounce green Chartreuse
- ½ ounce Luxardo maraschino liqueur
- ½ ounce freshly squeezed lime juice

Add all the ingredients to a cocktail shaker, fill with ice, and shake until the mixture is ice cold. Strain into a chilled cocktail glass.

Twentieth Century

- 1½ ounces gin
- ¾ ounce Lillet Blanc or Cocchi Americano
- ½ ounce white crème de cacao
- ¾ ounce freshly squeezed lemon juice
- Twist of lemon peel

Add the gin, Lillet Blanc, crème de cacao, and lemon juice to a cocktail shaker and fill with ice. Shake until the mixture is cold and strain (double strain if desired) into a chilled cocktail glass. Squeeze the lemon peel to spray the essential oils onto the surface of the drink. Use the peel as a garnish.

Aviation

- 1½ ounces gin
- ¾ ounce freshly squeezed lemon juice
- 2 dashes (½ teaspoon) maraschino liqueur
- 2 dashes (½ teaspoon) crème de violette
- Maraschino cherry, for garnish

Add the gin, lemon juice, maraschino liqueur, and crème de violette to a cocktail shaker filled with ice. Shake well until the mixture is very cold and then strain into a cocktail glass. Garnish the drink with the cherry and serve.

HOW TO MAKE A MARTINI

The martini [is] the only American invention as perfect
as the sonnet.

—H. L. MENCKEN

PEOPLE ASK ME WHY I stir a martini as opposed to
shaking it, and the answer is simple: clarity. If you shake a
cocktail, you end up with little bits of broken ice stuck in it.
These cause cloudiness, and, more tragically, they will quickly melt
and dilute the drink. The person making the martini will have a
difficult time taking this into account. The result: A minute or two
after being served, the ice melts and, darn it all, your shaken martini is too watery.

Stirring, on the other hand, leads to a cocktail that won't dilute any further once it's poured into a glass. And it will remain as
transparent as a mountain stream every step of the way.

Clarity is the martini's job. A well-made martini is clean and
elegant like a Japanese sword; you might not even mind so much
if it were the last thing you saw because it is such
a beautiful way to die.

> A WELL-MADE
> MARTINI IS CLEAN
> AND ELEGANT
> LIKE A JAPANESE
> SWORD

And it's fitting that a martini ought to be as
clear as glass because, culturally speaking, we use
it as an empty vessel. It's the generic cocktail in
Western symbology, a blankness onto which we
project countless ideas and aspirations. The martini
is, above all, not just a cocktail, it's a symbol for
what cocktails mean. In the book *Martini, Straight Up*, Lowell Ed-
munds enumerates a litany of messages that we're all crystal clear

about even if we never openly express them: The martini is sophisticated. It is optimistic. It is a drink of the past (and somehow always was a drink of the past). It stands for urban life, devil-may-care abandon, glamor. And unless the person holding it is James Bond—who was dead wrong about the whole matter of shaking versus stirring, you'll note—the martini stands for Americanness.

Many people have a general familiarity with the idea of a martini without knowing what one tastes like. When they take that virgin sip, they discover that the martini is not just one of the best-known cocktails, it's also one of the least forgiving. The standard reaction is a recoil and a grimace. "It's all booze!" the poor novice exclaims. (And what did you expect?)

But all of this is more useful to the screenwriter or novelist than it is to the drinker. Aren't we concerned about the practical applications here? What is a martini really for?

Once again the answer is clarity. The martini is not softened by any sweetness—there's no sweet vermouth, as in a Manhattan. Nor is there sugar, as in an old fashioned. So the first sip hits you like a cold block of ice to the face. Feeling clear yet? Science has yet to furnish us with a more efficient way to signal to your body that you mean to get down to serious business. It doesn't matter what kind of business—romance, danger, or maybe actual, literal business—the martini will prepare you. Normally I pooh-pooh the notion that different alcoholic drinks affect the body in different ways, but I don't know of any other cocktail that actually increases alertness like the martini seems to do.

Well, the first one does, anyway. Dorothy Parker had a terrific ditty about the martini's efficiency of attack:

I like to have a martini,
Two at the very most.
After three I'm under the table,
after four I'm under my host.

Before we go further, we have to run over some definitions to make sure everyone's absolutely clear on what we're talking about when we discuss the martini.

A martini consists of gin and vermouth, is stirred until ice cold, and may contain orange bitters. Several garnishes are permitted, including an olive, lemon twist, or pickled cocktail onion. (Why do I exclude olive brine, a commonplace additive? Say it with me again: *clarity.* You ruin a martini by clouding it with olive brine. Also, you may note that olive juice clashes badly with a lot of the fancy new gins out there, but go ahead and try it if you don't believe me.)

Some impostors going by the name martini are pretty laughable, so let's take a brief moment to laugh at them. A so-called chocolate martini is not a martini, it is a dessert. A blue martini is not a martini, it is a joke. None of the sugary martinis on the back page of a family restaurant menu are actually martinis. Those are training wheels for beginners who heard about martinis from television and want to try one, but couldn't possibly handle the real thing.

What about vodka? Feh. There's such a thing as a vodka martini—I suppose I can at least acknowledge its existence—but a vodka martini is not the original or anything close to the ideal. A vodka martini is the chicken burger to the gin martini's cheeseburger: second-rate and everyone knows it.

What makes a martini really click is the interplay between the pinelike bouquet of gin against the smooth texture and lightly spiced sweetness of fresh vermouth. Put them together and you get a cocktail of sublime subtlety and balance. Drop everything and just focus on the drink, lest you miss out on its Zen-like perfection and simplicity. One sip reminds you of orange peel and lemon-grass, the next conjures salt water and lavender. The floral notes (present mainly when you use good gin), the coldness, and the alcoholic thrust of a martini cleanse the spirit, the mind, and the palate like a deep inhalation of brisk autumn air, instantly flushing away the psychic grime that accumulates over a tough week. It can be administered before, during, and after grueling situations. To the mid-twentieth-century American salaryman, a martini was, paradoxically, both the apex of civilization and the purest antidote to civilization's stresses and ennui.

A vodka martini, by contrast, is cold ethanol and water in a glass. Tastes like booze, acts like booze. If you don't like gin, you're really missing out on what a martini is.

If you're with me on the gin proposition, here's how to proceed. The recipe is a fraught thing to commit to words because the composition of a martini has evolved over time, and in my opinion not really for the better. People nowadays expect a martini to be quite dry—which means light on the vermouth. I blame Winston Churchill. He apparently declared, circa the 1940s, that he liked his martinis without vermouth. He believed it was sufficient to bow in the direction of France while preparing one or just to touch a vermouth bottle, depending on which version of the story you hear. Fashion followed, and the standard martini went from dry to bone dry. When someone asks for a bone-dry martini they're basically just ordering cold gin. I personally think that's missing the point. I believe a martini should employ vermouth so that it feels round on the tongue; prepare it with gin alone and it feels thin and sharp.

Every martini drinker swears by a personal formula, and most will go out of their way to tell you all about theirs. There's an old joke about that. If you ever crash-land on a deserted island, look around and see if you have the makings of a martini on hand. If so, begin to fix one. As soon as you do, every asshole and his cousin will pop out from the woods and try to tell you that you're doing it wrong. You're saved!

All of which is to say this formula, my personal formula, is one of many possible "right" ways. Use it as a starting point.

Wet, Correct Martini

- 2 ounces quality gin
- Generous ½ ounce fresh dry vermouth, or more to taste
- 1–2 dashes orange bitters
- Twist of lemon peel, for garnish

Fill a mixing glass about halfway with fresh-smelling ice and add the gin and vermouth. Add 1 dash of orange bitters this time, try 2 dashes next time around, and take note of whether you prefer one or two. Stir the liquid until ice cold and strain into a chilled cocktail glass. Squeeze the lemon peel twist above the glass to spray the essential oils onto the surface of the drink. Slip the lemon peel into the drink, or otherwise arrange artfully.

Some notes on the recipe: This formula is going to look quite wet indeed to most people—that's old-time bar lingo for "heavy on vermouth"—but that's how they did it a century ago. And when the early twentieth century speaks to us about cocktails, we ought to at least listen. It knows more about the subject than we do. All the same, you might prefer something a bit drier; do experiment with less vermouth to see what you prefer (or, indeed, try more: A martini with a 2:1 ratio of gin to fresh vermouth is not bad at all).

Finally and most important, when you're choosing a gin for a martini, your guiding principle should be the more juniper flavored, the better. A big, oily, piney gin blossoms quite seductively in a martini. On the relatively affordable end, Beefeater or Broker's are my go-to choices. Tanqueray works well, too. If you have more expensive gin, say a luxurious $45 bottle you're not sure what to do with, show it off in a martini. If you can get them, try Green-hook (from Brooklyn), Victoria (from Victoria, B.C., Canada), or The Botanist (from Islay, Scotland).

When it comes to vermouth, my first choice is Noilly Prat—it has a sweetness that really works, even if the great Kingsley Amis dismissed it as too yellow in color—followed by Dolin dry, followed at a great distance by any other dry vermouth I've ever tried. You may note that my preferred brands are both French. Anything else is second best in a martini.

The orange bitters are an optional enhancement, yet one I strongly recommend. Orange bitters appeared in many martini recipes up until the 1930s and then they disappeared, and that's because they mostly stopped being manufactured. Now that orange bitters have come back to life in the twenty-first century—to

BASIC MARTINI LINGO

Martini: A cocktail consisting of gin, vermouth, and optional orange bitters. Vodka may be used in place of gin, but I don't recommend it.

Dry and wet: A *dry* martini contains relatively little vermouth, whereas a *wet* martini has more. By today's standards any martini that's more than about 15 percent vermouth is relatively wet.

Gibson: A martini with cocktail onions as garnish.

Up: A cocktail up or straight up means it's served cold and in a stemmed cocktail glass, with no additional ice.

Stirred: The proper way to prepare a martini—James Bond is wrong. Shaking makes the drink cloudy and overdiluted.

be found online or at your local gourmet food store—they're worth adding, because they bring complexity and zip. I think the orange plays nicely against the flavor of coriander seed, one of the "botanicals" that typically make up the flavor of gin. Any brand should be fine, but Regans' No. 6 orange bitters have a straightforwardly orangey flavor that works particularly well.

Regarding the finishing touch, namely, the garnish, you're probably used to an olive (or even a pickled onion, which makes a martini a **Gibson martini**). The olive is by far the preferable option to doodle on a bar napkin, or to use as a garnish if your martini is actually a neon sign that says "cocktails" on the bottom. The martini olive is an icon of cocktail lore and it looks cute. However, try it against the lemon twist in a taste test, and I bet you'll stick with the citrus. Lemon enjoys a small flavor advantage at frigid temperatures, and its advantage only improves over olives as the drink warms up. Don't worry, you can still have olives—as a snack on the side.

Finally, what to do for music? John Coltrane. Done.

VODKA IS OVER

Vodka is tasteless going down, but it is memorable coming up.

—GARRISON KEILLOR

IN CASE YOU DIDN'T KNOW, many cocktail and spirits snobs turn their noses up at vodka, and you vodka lovers out there won't get a lot of sympathy from me. While vodka may continue to outsell all the other spirits globally regardless of my own arm-flailing rants, I'd like to help at least a few people realize they can do better—and, frankly, deserve better—than this most soulless and pallid of liquids. I offer five reasons you should at least take a break from vodka while you get accustomed to other liquors. I'll try to be as polite as I can.

1. **It's fucking boring.** Vodka is to mixology as chicken breasts are to cuisine: the safe, predictable, dull choice. It's essentially just ethanol and water. You could make it in a laboratory, and chemistry students do. Good luck trying that with Scotch.

   Yes, there are small differences between brands. Polish rye vodkas seem especially nice to me. I picked Belvedere over the other vodkas in a blind taste test once; it has a hint of rye spice.

   The differences are subtle, however, and vodka is always quite plain. Don't let vodka connoisseurs—yes, such a tribe exists—persuade you that they're very significant. To a great extent, vodka is vodka.

2. **Vodka is usually a waste of an opportunity to drink something more interesting.** Imagine you have apprenticed under some renowned pizza maker in Naples for a year,

slaving away slicing ingredients while sweating next to a hot oven. You've spent long nights reading up on the history of pizza. You talk about pizza; dream about pizza. You're obsessed.

Ready to fly on your own, you return to your home country, buy a top-of-the-line wood-burning oven, and open for business. You proudly await the first customers salivating for authentic Neapolitan pie.

Except some rube walks in and says: "Uh, can you serve us something with a stuffed crust?"

Well, no. Not here. Not in the best, most authentic pizzeria in town.

This is much the same thing as ordering a vodka and soda at someone's awesome, carefully thought out cocktail bar. Stuffed-crust pizza may have its time and place (hangover Sunday, your couch), but there are occasions where you want to aim higher. A vodka and soda is simply not a special-occasion drink. If you're in a fancy cocktail bar, order something fancy. You'll drink better, look smarter, and make your bartender happier. And a little oak or juniper won't kill you, so try a whiskey or gin drink.

3. **Because dominating the 1990s and 2000s was enough.** Even if you do truly appreciate vodka for its simplicity or whatever, I would argue we've all had enough of it over recent decades. Let's move on to new experiences.

4. **Vodka is mostly the product of marketing, not love.** With some notable exceptions, vodka manufacturing can be characterized as an industrial process. Other spirits are made in a fashion more characteristic of artisanal production. When you're making, say, a whiskey or brandy, you need to have a talented distiller around and an experienced cooper who really knows the barrel-making business. It's a craft. Then you sell it on the basis of flavor.

It's a fairly straightforward process to make vodka, which is not aged. Then you hire a marketing agency to sell it. And what do you have to go on? A manufactured image: possibly a celebrity brand ambassador, a reassuringly high (and unjustifiable) price point, a cool bottle and/or name. Flavor is peripheral to the exercise. Becoming a fashionable brand is paramount.

5. **Because some of the reasons you tell yourself you drink vodka are wrong anyway.** Though there are some reports that this will start to change soon in certain countries, spirits generally don't include nutrition labels. Myths and ignorance always expand to fill a void, and in the case of spirits, there is now a widespread but deeply incorrect belief going around that vodka contains fewer calories than other spirits. In fact, 45 milliliters (about 1½ ounces) of 40% spirit contains 97 calories whether you're sipping tequila, gin, rum, vodka, or whiskey. (Sugar adds more calories, so a sweetened spirit like spiced rum or flavored whiskey will have a little bump above the others.)

What about vodka as a solution for food sensitivities? Some celiac sufferers have told me they drink vodka but not whiskey because the former is made from potatoes and the latter from grain.

Wrong again: Most vodka is made from grain, too. Absolut, Grey Goose, Smirnoff, Stolichnaya—name the vodka bottle on your liquor shelf, and chances are high it's made from grain. If it doesn't say how a vodka is made on the back label, look it up online. Potato vodkas are actually relatively rare. Examples include Chopin with the black cap, and Karlsson's Gold. Tito's, meanwhile, is made from corn. Incidentally, I've also heard celiac sufferers say they drink gin because of their condition. Well, the vast majority of gin is distilled from grain, too.

The second reason it's misguided to drink vodka as a celiac solution: Distillation doesn't carry gluten, which is a protein, over into the final product. I'm neither a doctor nor a biochemist, so take this as information rather than advice, but distilling involves collecting the vapor off a bubbling vat of fermented liquid, separating it from the solids. Distillation is all about collecting alcohol in the form of condensation and discarding the rest. Think of it this way: Distilled spirits should not contain the offending proteins from the wheat and barley any more than the dirt from behind your ears ends up in the water droplets on your bathroom mirror after you take a shower.

Granted, there may be some grain dust in the air at the distillery that sneaks into the liquid when it's poured into barrels or bottled. In part because of this possibility, I am told it's quite difficult to get a spirit declared gluten-free. Few spirit makers bother. But if you really want to be safe from gluten, opt for a Caribbean rum (made from molasses), tequila (made from agave), or brandy (made from grapes or other fruit). Whiskey, gin, and vodka are equally dangerous—which is to say probably not very, but avoid them all if you're being cautious.

BUT WHEN WE DO POUR VODKA . . .

I do believe vodka has a place in the drinker's repertoire, albeit a small one. Go ahead and have it with raw oysters and/or caviar (though I'd personally rather have a dry—fino or manzanilla—sherry with either, or stout with the oysters. See? There's usually a more flavorful way to go).

At home, most of my vodka supply is for the sake of guests. The odd time I pick up a bottle, I go for good old Stolichnaya (original, red label), which is a bit medicinal tasting but does the job. When it's available I stock up on the fiery, peppery Blackwoods, from Scotland. I also like Finlandia. Belvedere is the most interesting common vodka, as I mentioned earlier, but the stuff is expensive. Go for it if it's in your budget. I don't waste money on expensive vodka.

Moscow Mule

How about a cocktail? The Moscow mule was invented in 1940s Los Angeles, the result of a joint and mutually beneficial brainwave between a U.S. importer of Smirnoff vodka and a businessman who was bringing in ginger beer. While hardly anyone drinks them now, Moscow mules helped make vodka popular in America in the 1950s. The copper mugs that seem to exist solely for the purpose of serving Moscow mules are popping up again in stores, so maybe the drink is staging a comeback, too.

- 2 ounces vodka
- 4–6 ounces ginger beer
- ½ ounce freshly squeezed lime juice
- Lime wedge and/or mint sprig, for garnish

Fill a Collins glass or Moscow mule mug with ice. Pour in the vodka, fill nearly to the top with ginger beer, and then add the lime juice to finish it off. Garnish with the lime wedge or decorate with the spent lime shell; maybe toss a sprig of mint in there, too.

OTHER WHITE SPIRITS

The spirits I discuss here will occupy a niche space in the drinker's diet, if they have any place at all. Here's a quick introduction in case you do run into them.

AKVAVIT

Scandinavia's answer to vodka is always infused with spice. Caraway and dill are typical. Akvavit (also spelled *aquavit* and called "snaps" in Denmark) is served chilled in small glasses. While it's reportedly fading from popularity in its homelands, akvavit remains popular around Christmas, and I suspect the hipsters will pedal over the horizon and rescue it any day now.

The lovely Norwegian brand Linie is stored in barrels in the hold of a ship and taken on a little ocean journey for aging, which lends it a bit of character and makes a fun little story to tell.

Trident

Cocktail author and blogger Robert Hess invented the trident cocktail, which showcases akvavit; I believe it's destined to be one of the few cocktail creations of our time that will be remembered in the future. You may find that each sip is different—one woody, the next herbal, the next sweet and tart like fresh cherries. It's a little odd and requires a quartet of unusual ingredients but the results are worth it.

- 1 ounce akvavit
- 1 ounce Cynar (an Italian digestif that includes artichoke)
- 1 ounce dry sherry (look for a manzanilla or fino sherry)
- 2 dashes peach bitters
- Twist of lemon peel

Add the akvavit, Cynar, sherry, and bitters to a mixing glass with ice and stir until the mixture is well chilled. Strain into a chilled cocktail glass. Squeeze the lemon peel to spray the essential oils onto the surface of the drink, then discard.

GRAPPA

Until just a few years ago, most grappa went around smelling like feet. Then grappa makers witnessed the successful revival of formerly bumpkin spirits like shochu and bourbon and decided to class up their act, improving production and marketing tactics. If all you've ever sampled are the regrettable grappas of yesteryear, today's récherché single-grape and single-estate grappas might knock your socks off.

SOJU AND SHOCHU

Soju is from Korea and shochu is from Japan, often lumped together (including here) due to geography and the similarity of their names, plus the fact that both liquors can be distilled from rice, though shochu also comes from barley (yes, please) or sweet potatoes (uh, you first).

Korea's national spirit, soju, is light tasting and served cold. In strength and temperament it is somewhere between sake and shochu. It's sometimes proffered as liquid courage at the karaoke parlor. It will be smooth even if you aren't.

Shochu has been a common person's drink in Japan since at least 1559, when people working on a village temple carved the beams with graffiti, complaining that the priest in charge of the works didn't supply the expected hooch. What you're after is mugi shochu, which is made from barley. Mix with grapefruit soda or just serve on the rocks. The Japanese archipelago of Okinawa specializes in a weapons-grade shochu relative called awamori, which has, on multiple occasions, knocked me—a fairly experienced drinker (not to brag, just saying)—sideways faster than a karate chop to the temple. If you encounter it, exercise extreme caution.

PISCO

Pisco is a pale South American brandy with a mild, interesting flavor, sweeter and not much more challenging than vodka. It most frequently appears in the pisco sour, a tart and frothy cousin of the daiquiri.

Pisco Sour

- 1 egg white
- 1½ ounces pisco
- ¾ ounce freshly squeezed lemon or lime juice, by preference
- 1 ounce simple syrup
- A few generous drops of Angostura bitters (or totally geek out and order Peruvian Amargo Chuncho bitters)

Shake the egg white in a cocktail shaker without ice until frothy ("dry shake"). Add ice, pisco, lemon juice, and simple syrup. Shake vigorously again for at least 20 seconds, and strain into a chilled cocktail glass. Drop the bitters in an attractive pattern on the surface of the froth.

EAUX DE VIE

Most European countries produce clear distillations of fruit—called brandies, eaux de vie, rakis, or something else. Even the back-woods stuff can be impressive. A friend smuggled me home a bit of her Hungarian uncle's pálinka. The distillate exhibited obvious virtuosity, with none of the oily or nail polish aromas that can mar a home-distilled spirit. The lesson: Should someone's hairy-armed European uncle hand you a glass of something clear that he made himself, it might not kill you to try it.

KNOW YOUR WHISKEY

There is no bad whiskey. There are only some whiskeys that
aren't as good as others.

—UNKNOWN

PLENTY OF PEOPLE LEARN when they're young
how to order a well-known, affordable brand of whiskey
with a mixer at the bar—say, Jack Daniel's, Canadian Club,
or Dewar's with cola or ginger ale. But venture further into the
world of whiskey? They dare not. When they come to my apart-
ment and I offer them a glass of something slightly more expensive
with a splash of water, they often blanch and raise their hands in
an "I'm sorry" gesture. "I don't really know anything about whiskey," they say, as if that disqualifies them from trying.

How do they think I learned a few things? Certainly not by
refusing a glass.

A glass of whiskey is not a helicopter; you're not going to
cause a fiery catastrophe if you grab the apparatus without prior
training. Relax. Take the glass.

Perhaps some familiarity will help diminish the fears. I'd be
willing to bet that most people don't have a clue what whiskey
actually *is*. Nor do they realize whiskey (which is
spelled *whisky* in the Commonwealth and Japan) is a
term that comprises a few closely related spirits.
Whiskey is just grain alcohol aged in oak. And in case
you didn't know—don't feel bad if you didn't; it's not
common knowledge—rye, bourbon, and Scotch are
all *varieties* of whiskey.

> WHISKEY IS
> JUST GRAIN
> ALCOHOL AGED
> IN OAK.

Whiskey is distilled from a fermented grain liquid that's essentially a form of beer, albeit one that's specifically made for the purpose of whiskey making. No one would actually drink it for its own sake. At the Laphroaig distillery in Scotland, where the distiller's beer is milky-pale and tastes of ashes, a sip of it nearly caused me to lose my breakfast. The grains in the distiller's beer vary depending on region and can include barley (malted or plain), rye, wheat, and occasionally other grains, such as millet and triticale.

When this beer (or "mash," in the case of bourbon) is distilled two or three times, it produces a white spirit. Like the devil, this powerful, sulfurous white liquor goes by many names: Americans call it bald face, white dog, or white lightning, while Canadians and Scottish distillers call it new make. In some contexts you'll see baby whiskey referred to rather prosaically as distillate. And if it's illegal—or produced by certain hipster-oriented U.S. craft distilleries—it's called moonshine. Likewise, in Ireland, poitín (pronounced pot-CHEEN) is either illegal or hipster. Finally, you see the term white whiskey on a few American products.

Most people find unaged whiskey too "hot" and exuberant. Distillers figured out in the nineteenth century that a long slumber in wood mellows spirits and makes them taste yummy, and the discovery changed whiskey for the better. To protect the public from the tongue-prickling shock of young distillate, in Canada, Ireland, and the United Kingdom it's illegal to put the word *whiskey* on the bottle unless the spirit has aged at least three years in oak.

Barrels made from different oak species give you different effects, and the whiskey will also suck out any traces of the liquids the barrel held during a previous life. Whereas bourbon must be made with fresh new barrels every time, which helps account for the boldness of its flavor, for Canadian, Irish, and Scotch whiskeys, recycled barrels are the norm. The distillers buy used barrels from bourbon makers, as well as sherry bodegas (and, less commonly, other sources). Contact with the inside of a barrel over a period of years allows the distillate to leach flavorful chemicals called congeners from the wood. This effect is thought to be responsible for at least 70 percent of the flavor in whiskey—its characteristic palette of vanilla and caramel, even fruit and spice—and a good portion of the resulting hangovers, too. (I'm not certain how they came up with the 70 percent flavor figure, but I hear it often it on distillery tours.)

There are several whiskey-producing countries and styles to be discovered, but three general families dominate the landscape. The Irish invented whiskey, but that country's version isn't any more old fashioned than the others', as it continued to evolve in the twentieth century. Today most Irish whiskey is made in a relatively gentle, approachable style. Next we have Scotch, which is the term for whisky made in Scotland according to certain rules. It's the jazz of the family: diverse, and equal parts challenging and rewarding, and thus a magnet for snobbery. We usually lump Japanese whisky into the same category as Scotch because it's largely a mimic of the Scottish style—and many feel the apprentice has matched the master. Third and finally, we have the multiheaded beast of North America, which consists of bourbon and its sibling, Tennessee whiskey, as well as American rye and Canadian whisky (which is also sometimes called "rye" in Canada, but we'll get to that).

So those are the basics. But you can't sell a product with a plodding discussion of how different grains react in a fermenting vat. You need mystery, romance; you have to weave a story. And the story of whiskey, broadly speaking and broadly true, is that of a backwoods homemade liquor that its makers gradually elevated into a craft.

Whereas gin is the quintessential cosmopolitan spirit, made from ingredients gathered from every inhabited latitude and usually presented as urban and modern, whiskey has sometimes been portrayed as a rural liquor, especially in the United States. Whiskey as we know it was pioneered (and is often still made) in backcountry spots from Kentucky to Craigellachie, out-of-the-way places where the moonshine makers of yesteryear could hide from the probing eye of the taxman. Whiskey is still often presented with associations to the outdoors and rural life, even if the principal market has long been city folk.

Whiskey is also invariably presented to the consumer as the product of generations of tradition. Brands will even feign a heritage when they have none.

The rarefied air that whiskey enjoys today is amusing when you think about the fact that it evolved from moonshine around the late eighteenth century. One thing has remained constant: From the days of half-desperate Irish peasants in their rough-spun tunics to today's traders in bespoke suits, it seems people have always regarded whiskey as a high-alcohol stress reliever, a means of escape. Whereas once it was merely strong stuff meant to soften the hard knocks of preindustrial life, nowadays whiskey has evolved into a tastier, easier-drinking spirit prized for the way it couples power and nuance in each beautiful brown sip. A whiskey is something to cap a day worth remembering—or forgetting. Scotch, Japanese, and Irish whiskeys are especially suited to slow sipping, the better to underscore a celebratory and/or contemplative moment. There exist a few cocktails that showcase them as well, and many people simply add ice and club soda to make a highball.

Cocktails are where rye whiskey and Canadian whisky shine, although you can sip the better examples neat as well. Bourbon is either a cocktail whiskey or a sippin' whiskey and excels in either job.

An air of outlaw cred and machismo and the hunting lodge still cling to whiskey, which I'm sure has contributed to the deeply ingrained hesitation the average person has around it, especially a lot of women. Certain people value whiskey as a talisman of masculinity, and to let women into the club would risk abjuring the manly magic.

Well, too bad. As always, I say there's no such thing as a gendered drink, and only little boys need a no-girls-allowed club.

Speaking of magic, even among men there's a sense that some of us have been touched by the heavens with a special ability to appreciate whiskey. I once read a preface to a whiskey book that effectively said: "The fella who wrote this book? Palate of the gods. Nose like a bloodhound. Few can appreciate whisky like he does."

How off-putting is that? How antidemocratic? Why would the ordinary person even bother trying whiskey if it's implied that most of us could never ascend to the pinnacle of its appreciation anyway? The message isn't even true: Everything I know about drinks education and the biology of the human senses suggests that the "ability" to appreciate the nuances of whiskey is a function of experience, not an innate power.

Let's not let snobbery and made-up demographic prejudices keep anyone away from whiskey. Its rightful place is as a drink of the people, and that means you.

THREE GENERAL POINTERS ABOUT WHISKEY

Even if you're not destined to fall down the rabbit hole of whiskey geekery, here are three basic pointers to bear in mind.

1. **Great whiskey doesn't have to be expensive.** Whenever I refer to "affordable brands," I'm careful to make sure it's a statement of fact, not a slight.

   Cheap whiskey has many uses, and I promise you that anyone who says otherwise does not know what he's talking about. Call his bluff. "I don't know, I find The Famous Grouse goes down really nicely for the money, don't you?" There's no comeback for that because it's true.

   I keep a mental list of go-to inexpensive whiskeys in every whiskey subcategory. Keep reading for recommendations. If you're going to make whiskey a big part of your life, you're going to want to have some throwaway-but-tasty stuff you can grab a slug of without any sense of occasion. You also need cheap whiskey for those times when you just want to splash some mixer in with it.

Finally, cheap whiskey is handy for making punch. Or for throwing parties in general: It's a rookie move to give your guests clearance to decimate your top-shelf supply. I'm still wondering what happened to my last bottle of Glenfiddich 21. Reserve the good whiskey for quieter times with a small group, ideally your nearest and dearest. When the party's gently ramping up or down, that's the time to bring out the special bottle. If you're fool enough to give your friend's obnoxious cousin that last drop of Pappy Van Winkle, maybe you didn't deserve it in the first place.

2. **No matter what you see on television or what you see other people doing, you probably don't want to drink whiskey on the rocks.** Only a purist would say you should *never, ever* try whiskey on the rocks, but if you really want to taste what's going on, try it neat first. Then add a splash of water. Ice makes whiskey cold, and coldness kills a lot of the nuance of flavor. I go over this point in more detail in the next chapter.

3. **Having said that, there's no right or wrong. You just enjoy what you enjoy.** There may be countless whiskey reviews out there, and awards for the "best," but you're always free to ignore all that and drink what you like. And besides, quality is surprisingly consistent in the world of whiskey, at least among the brands marketed to industrialized countries. You rarely crack open a true stinker. Should you be handed something you don't enjoy, yet social convention insists that you have some, try hiding it under some ginger ale or another mixer and see if that makes the medicine easier to take.

MAJOR WHISKEY STYLES: A HANDY CHART

STYLE	POPULAR BRANDS	GRAINS	BARRELS USED FOR AGING	USES AND NOTES
Bourbon	Jim Beam, Wild Turkey	At least 51 percent corn (maize), plus barley (malted), wheat, and/or rye	Must be freshly charred American oak	For sippin', cocktails, or with a mixer. Must be made in America but not necessarily in Kentucky
Tennessee whiskey	Jack Daniel's, George Dickel	At least 51 percent corn, plus rye and barley (malted)	Must be freshly charred American oak	Differs from bourbon only in terms of filtration through charcoal, and it must be made in Tennessee
Rye whiskey (American)	Rittenhouse, Sazerac	At least 51 percent rye, usually higher; recipe filled out with the same grains as bourbon	Must be freshly charred American oak	Mostly for cocktails
Single malt Scotch	Glenfiddich, The Glenlivet	100 percent malted barley	Ex–bourbon barrels (the most typical option), ex–sherry butts, or a combination thereof; sometimes other types of barrels are used for finishing (such as rum or French oak)	Sipping, with spring water. Rarely used in cocktails (but it's okay to do so no matter what purists say)

STYLE	POPULAR BRANDS	GRAINS	BARRELS USED FOR AGING	USES AND NOTES
Blended Scotch	Johnnie Walker, The Famous Grouse	Features a mixture of single malt Scotches for flavor, though the majority of the volume is plainer grain whiskey made with corn, wheat, and unmalted barley	Same situation as single malt Scotch	Sipping with spring water, or with mixers. Sometimes used in cocktails
Japanese whisky	Yamazaki, Hibiki	Single malts and blends produced in a similar fashion to Scotch	Barrel practices similar to those of Scotch, plus the native Japanese oak species mizunara is used to make barrels as well	Serving is generally the same as with Scotch, though serving with ice and water at the same time is common during hot Japanese summers
Irish whiskey	Bushmills, Jameson	100 percent malted barley for single malts, combination of malted and unmalted barley for single pot still. Most Irish whiskey, however, is blended and produced in similar fashion to blended Scotch	Barrel practices similar to those of Scotch	Best if sipped with a splash of spring water. Doing as a shot is common as well, but not recommended if you want to actually taste the quality

STYLE	POPULAR BRANDS	GRAINS	BARRELS USED FOR AGING	USES AND NOTES
Canadian whisky	Crown Royal, Canadian Club	Various combinations of corn, rye, barley (malted and unmalted), occasionally wheat, and triticale	Mostly ex–bourbon barrels, some freshly charred barrels made of American oak; occasional use of ex–sherry butts and other special barrels for flavor	Usually mixed with ginger ale or cola, or mixed into cocktails. Some brands contain a lot of rye, others little or none; either way, Canadians call their own domestic whisky "rye"

How to
Appreciate Scotch
(and Japanese) Whisky

Freedom an' whiskey gang thegither.

—ROBERT BURNS

I love scotch. Scotchy scotch scotch.

—RON BURGUNDY

WHETHER YOU LOVE THE STUFF or recoil in disgust at the very thought of it, think back to your first sip of Scotch. Did the smell alone make you consider releasing a little barf? I'll wager it did. Ah, the gloriously fetid things Scotch whisky can taste like to a novice: swamp water, spoiled cheese, stinky feet. The first time I stole some Chivas Regal from the family liquor cabinet, I wondered why anyone would drink it. (Granted, I still wonder why anyone would drink Chivas Regal 12.) It's taken countless nights, a lot of tastings, and, frankly, a bit of a love affair with the stuff to go from gagging on stolen sips to regarding a dram by the fire as one of the three or four best things in life.

The Scots have been making whisky for centuries, but Scotch as we know it—the daunting liquor with an air of luxury—is much younger than that. When an infestation of phylloxera hit the French wine industry in the 1860s, cognac's bad fortune was an opportunity for Scotch whisky: Brandy and cigars had long served as the genteel after-dinner treat for Western men, and something had to step in to take brandy's place. Scotch was ready to take over, especially since blending had recently been legalized, which allowed purveyors of whisky to mix different malt and grain whiskies together to make Scotch palatably smooth. Even the French took it up, and they remain the world's biggest Scotch drinkers per capita.

Today, Scotch reigns as the king of spirits (sorry, cognac, but it's true), popular worldwide and in more demand than the relatively tiny and quaint industry can keep up with. The law of supply and demand is one of the factors one might use to justify the exorbitant sum that Scotch can fetch. It's also expensive to age. Think of all the thousands of nights that the barrel sleeps in a warehouse, watched over by security guards.

I find the experience is usually worth the cost. If you subscribe to the belief that great art is that which rewards repeated consumption, no liquid beverage better qualifies for the distinction than Scotch. It's a slow, contemplative beverage to be savored and mentally picked apart. Every sniff has the potential to reveal fresh nuance; each sip is like a new vantage point on a beautiful sculpture. You taste honey one moment, seaweed the next. Scotch forces you to slow down and appreciate the moment. That is its greatest gift.

> SCOTCH FORCES YOU TO SLOW DOWN AND APPRECIATE THE MOMENT. THAT IS ITS GREATEST GIFT.

What a shame that unfamiliarity and fear of embarrassment keep this nirvana in a glass from reaching more people's lips. It's not just the flavor and cost of Scotch whisky that make it scary, it's the cloak of pretension that usually surrounds it. Scotch was invented centuries ago by poor crofters and moonshiners, but you wouldn't know it by seeing how it's revered in our time. A well-aged bottle can sell for tens of thousands of dollars and be described approvingly as redolent of baked oatcakes, heather blossoms, and a pleasant flutter of hickory smoke. The fuss that surrounds Scotch appreciation resembles the world of wine, but with plaid and bagpipes and, frankly, a bit of old man smell. Kingsley Amis wrote in 1983 that "on present trends there'll be whisky snobs fit to compare with any wine snobs of yesteryear," and if he didn't quite live to see that prophecy fulfilled, we certainly have.

I can understand why someone would be intimidated. The thing to remember is that no one—and I mean no one—is born already loving Scotch.

Let's demystify it a little here. *Scotch* is just a short way of saying "Scotch whisky," which is defined as any whisky distilled and aged in Scotland. As a further requirement, it has to be aged for at least three years in oak following distillation. This basic legal formula leaves ample latitude for interpretation: What kind of oak should the distiller use, American or Spanish? (Once again, Scotch is always aged in barrels that were first used for something else, typically bourbon or sherry.) Should the distillery malt the barley over old-fashioned, stinky peat smoke or use neutral-smelling dry heat? What shape should the stills be, and how many times should the whisky be distilled? Different answers to these questions yield different final products. From a chemistry standpoint, every whisky is a unique soup of aldehydes, fatty acids, esters, and alcohols in an ethanol-water solution. Some of these chemicals are created during the distillation process. Later, the alcohol sucks other molecules out of the barrel during the long slumber of maturation. That vanilla flavor you may detect, for example, is actually vanillin, a phenolic aldehyde that's abundant in American white oak as well as in the familiar vanilla bean. Because it's the same chemical, you really are smelling vanilla in that glass of Scotch, in a sense.

Then there's the distinction between single malt Scotch versus blended Scotch. Single malt is the product of a single distillery and considered pretty posh. Blends combine malted Scotch from various distilleries with relatively plain grain whisky. Blends are usually (but not always) more affordable than single malt, and often held in less esteem nowadays. Single malt Scotch is, perhaps counterintuitively, the newer product category. Very little of the stuff existed before the 1960s, and it really took off as a worldwide phenomenon in the 1980s and after.

You could think of honey if you're trying to grasp the difference between the two kinds of Scotch. Single malt is like fancy farmers' market honey from a single locale. The purveyors are keen to tell you every detail about how it was made. Blends are like the honey you buy from a supermarket, which was gathered from many places and then blended for consistency. The identities of the Scotches that go into a blended whisky, and the ratios involved, are subject to variation from batch to batch and are kept secret, or secret-ish. You're not encouraged to ask too many questions, just like you'd have a hard time nailing down the origins of the honey that goes into the plastic bear at the grocery store.

There are also blended malt whiskies that are made up of only different single malts and do not contain any grain whisky; these are rare (Poit Dhubh is one fine example, and there's Taketsuru from Japan) and can be considered just as premium as single malts.

There are around a hundred single malt distilleries and at least that number again of blended brands (before you even start to count the cheapo store brands at UK supermarkets). The dizzying diversity of Scotch is what beguiles the geeks and bewilders the uninitiated. But there's absolutely no social harm in asking for advice if you need it. Very few people can be handed a pages-long list of whiskies at a specialty bar and truthfully claim to know their GlenDronachs from their Glenlivets. To show humility and curiosity is to show maturity, and maturity is what makes a Scotch drinker of you. Scotch is almost the epitome of an acquired taste; a rite of passage into adulthood—a potentially daunting one that some people never get around to trying, like moving out of Mom's basement.

If you've only ever taken an exploratory sip of Scotch and been tempted to spit it out, try this next time: Make it four Scotches instead of one. Line up a few different brands and try them one by one, and slowly, according to the procedure I outline later in this chapter. The objective is to find the Scotch that strikes you as the least objectionable. That's a start. From there, you can begin to figure out what you actually like, and maybe even start to fall in love. Knowing just one popular Scotch that you can order and enjoy is infinitely preferable to not knowing any. And you'll be surprised how quickly you progress from disgust to tolerance to delight.

This procedure worked for me, too. The first time I actually enjoyed Scotch, I was twenty-four years old and working in a pub in Lancashire, England. The William Grant & Sons regional sales rep came in to give the staff a whisky-tasting lesson, featuring the company's Grant's and Glenfiddich whiskies. Over the course of the session, I found myself actually enjoying the eighteen-year-old Glenfiddich, which was then called Ancient Reserve. I still admire it as a whisky and can see why I was entranced: It's a smooth customer, with loads of caramel and vanilla, and just peeking through all that is the pear aroma that's characteristic of all of Glenfiddich's whiskies.

I'm not being a wanker, I promise. I really can smell those things, and so can a lot of other Scotch lovers. The more you get used to it, the more you perceive the nuances of the aromas, the beauty in the differences, instead of a generalized "Scotchiness." You might not often think of drinking as an activity that requires persistence, but in the case of Scotch it might.

Also, don't let anyone try to persuade you that you're destined to be clueless about Scotch because you're young and/or female. Scotch is for everyone. The last time I performed the four-

Scotches trick, my apprentices were two fellow Canadians, twenty-something women. They were friends of my brother's who had recently moved to Scotland and were keen to learn a little about the local spirit. I was in Edinburgh for work, so we met up at a pub with a long whisky list. Every once in a while, an older man at the next table leaned over to give his unsolicited advice and opinions. He evidently felt that a Scotch lesson for two young women was some kind of mansplaining emergency that called for male reinforcements. Unless you're a man over thirty, this is likely to happen when you learn about Scotch, so be ready for it. For a less patronizing initial experience, it's worth checking if there are women-only Scotch-tasting nights at a whiskey bar where you live; these are increasingly common.

Meanwhile, you don't have to stress over being familiar with different distilleries and that sort of thing. Knowing a couple of brands is enough. You can hardly go too wrong anyway. Scotch whisky might be the most consistent category of booze in terms of quality: There are very few bad ones out on the market, especially in developed countries. For now, just focus on getting the stuff down your gullet and maybe appreciating it a little. As always with Scotch, the key is to go slow and enjoy yourself.

THE PROCEDURE FOR DRINKING

This is the best way I know for really tasting and savoring a Scotch. I first learned it in that pub in Lancashire, and I still do it more than a dozen years later. It's the manner in which most guided Scotch tastings are run because it allows you to carefully savor the aromas—and what's going on in your nose is the main event when it comes to whisky tasting (as opposed to your tongue, as in wine tasting). There are other ways to prepare and drink Scotch—with soda, on the rocks, even with cola, green tea, or coconut water—but for a truly contemplative experience, especially if you're trying to acquire the taste, this is what I recommend.

First, you'll need water. Spring water is ideal, distilled is acceptable, and even tap water will work if it's all you have on hand. Warning: fussy old Scotch hounds will grumble about tainting the whisky with chlorine if they catch you using tap water. But who cares?

Regarding glassware, you're probably used to seeing people drink Scotch in rocks glasses—ideally cut-crystal ones, or something comparably eye-catching—and these will work just fine if you have them. Most glasses would work acceptably well, come to think of it; don't bother fussing too much. What's the ideal? Something called the Glencairn glass, which was designed specifically for tasting Scotch. It's wider at the bottom and tapers inward, the idea being that it gathers the airborne aromatic compounds and waves them up your nose, much like a bowl-shaped wineglass is supposed to do.

Next, assemble the Scotch. The thing to do is serve up a few brands with rather different flavor characteristics to see what kind of Scotch most appeals to you. See my four flavor "teams," starting on page 150. Maybe pick one from each team, or at least cover three of the bases, and take note of which one you prefer.

When you're ready to drink, start by pouring a little whisky into your glass. Stick your nose in it. Open your mouth and inhale through your nose. You kind of look like an asshole right now and I'm sorry for that, but the opening-the-mouth thing really does help you smell fleeting images of flavors, which can appear and vanish in your consciousness like plot details of a dream you're trying to remember. Connoisseurs often talk about "nosing" whisky rather than "tasting" because smell can be more important than taste. The alcohol will deaden your taste buds, so the hints of hazelnut and violet and so on will come from your nose as opposed your tongue.

Next, sip the whisky. The tiniest of nips will do. Feel how it moves around in your mouth—is it silky-smooth or thin? Gentle or prickly? And what can you taste? Sure, it just tastes "Scotchy" at first, but some whiskies are spicy, others are sweet, some are both at the same time, and others strike you with the unmistakable acridity of smoke.

The most important part comes next: adding the water. Start with a few drops. Smell the whisky again. The water disrupts an equilibrium that had kept some sweeter, fruit-like aromas—long-chain esters, if you care to know the chemistry—below the surface. The water frees them and they will now waft into the air. The whisky can seem livelier and fruitier after water is added. If you like the effect, keep going. (Smoky flavors, meanwhile, can actually be dampened by adding water.)

Next, drink it down. Whereas people spit at a wine tasting, most actually swallow the stuff at a Scotch tasting. This gives them a chance to observe the heat and length of the finish. A great Scotch goes down long, warm, and spicy (the spicy flavors—Christmasy aromas like nutmeg and allspice in particular—often come from Spanish oak). What you probably don't want in a finish is short, hot, and harsh.

Now concentrate and see if you have a favorite whisky out of the ones you've tried. If not—if they all tasted gross to you—maybe Scotch isn't your thing. Taste buds change over a lifetime and you might learn to love it someday. Try again in a few years. In the meantime, please exit the ride here.

The rest of you will probably struggle to describe what you

drank. Comparisons will include basic observations like "this one was sweeter" or "lighter" or "stronger" or, of course, "smoky" or "not smoky." That's perfectly fine. You're finding your footing. And it really isn't necessary to develop a vocabulary for Scotch criticism in order to enjoy it anyway.

Once again, most people who try a few Scotches at one sitting come out with a preference, however weakly defined. The four teams I've defined could help you search for that whisky that really makes a Scotch drinker of you.

THE FOUR TEAMS

I admit I stole this idea from a cheesy whisky museum in Edinburgh. When I visited, guests were invited to use a scratch-and-sniff panel to see which of four flavor categories they enjoyed best. Needless to say, I suggest you use actual Scotch when trying to figure out what Scotch you like.

Sorting all the dizzying diversity of Scotch whisky into four distinct categories requires me to oversimplify the picture a great deal. Yet trying a whisky from each of these groups should prove a useful exercise for the Scotch learner. If you enjoy one whisky from each team, chances are high that you'll at least appreciate the others. Most of the brand suggestions here are relatively easy to find. If you're starting a collection, you could use this guide as a reference for ensuring you cover all the flavor bases and have a diversity of Scotches to offer your guests.

TEAM YELLOW

As a general rule, the relatively light Scotches of Team Yellow make for excellent drinking before dinner or in warm weather, while the other categories have a more overwhelming effect on the taste buds and are best reserved for chilly climes and after-dinner drinking.

BLENDS
Ballantine's Finest
Cutty Sark
Dewar's White Label

SINGLE MALTS
Auchentoshan
The Glenlivet 12
Glenmorangie Original
Rosebank
Glenkinchie

FROM JAPAN
Yamazaki 12
Hibiki

TEAM RED

Richer and more robust than Team Yellow, the Scotches in Team Red often feature a deep sweetness that reminds some people of dried fruits (raisins, prunes, and the like). In the finish—that is, when you finally swallow—you may pick up hints of wintry spices like nutmeg and clove. Glenfarclas, for example, has been advertised as "Christmas cake in a glass." These flavors can come from aging in former sherry barrels (officially called "butts") and sometimes can also be attributed to the whisky being run through stills that were built especially short and squat, which encourages oily flavors to be expressed during distillation.

BLENDS
The Famous Grouse
Grant's Sherry Cask
Mac Na Mara

SINGLE MALTS
The Balvenie DoubleWood
Glenfiddich 15
GlenDronach
Glenfarclas
Balblair
Glenturret
The Macallan (especially the darker-colored ones)

FROM JAPAN
Taketsuru
Yamazaki (older expressions)

TEAM BLUE

One of the major questions that can arise when offered a Scotch is: Do you like peated or not? If you like the whiskies in Team Blue best, your answer is, "Yes, but not too peaty." Whereas the sooty whiskies of Team Black are sometimes held to be the province of eccentrics, extremist foodies, and Swedes, a judicious dose of peat—as we encounter in Team Blue—can be considered an elegant touch.

If you can find it where you live, Té Bheag (it's pronounced "chay veck," not "tea bag," because Gaelic spelling is funny that way) makes a splendid, affordable everyday lightly peated blended whisky. If you can't find Té Bheag, splash out a little and buy yourself some Johnnie Walker Black instead. I'm confident you can find that one where you live, and, for that matter, on any spot on our planet where a week has seven days and the locals know what an American dollar bill looks like. Johnnie Black has reportedly been a favorite Scotch for everyone from the late Christopher Hitchens to bloodthirsty dictators and Middle Eastern sheikhs who like to take a nip on the sly. So if it turns out to be your favorite, you'll be in illustrious, if not entirely nice, company.

BLENDS

Johnnie Walker Black
Chivas Regal 18
Ballantine's 17
Té Bheag
White Horse
Black Bottle

SINGLE MALTS

Highland Park
Springbank
Longrow
Caol Ila
Talisker

FROM JAPAN

Nikka Yoichi (Get it while you can—while it should still kick around on the shelf for a few years, Nikka has announced the discontinuation of Yoichi single malt.)

TEAM BLACK

Scotches made from barley that's been malted in the traditional way—that is, in kilns heated with burning peat (swamp dirt, sort of)—are referred to as *peated*. These taste strange to novices. They're so funky that drinking them could almost seem like a culinary dare, like that coffee that passes through a cat's ass. People always smell the smoke first, which can call to mind things like seaweed and embalming fluid. Keep tasting till you get used to it, and the weird symphony of flavors becomes a joy—for some, anyway. My favorite substance in the cosmos is Lagavulin 16, which balances peaty iodine-and-campfire aromas against peppery, peachy sherry cask.

The Western Scottish island of Islay is famous around the world for making several of the smoke-infused whiskies.

BLENDS

The Black Grouse

(Alas, that's it. Johnnie Walker Double Black is almost, but not quite, smoky enough to belong here, and the Black Bottle brand, popular in the UK, was recently reformulated to be less peaty, to the dismay of smoky Scotch freaks.)

SINGLE MALTS

Laphroaig

Ardbeg

Lagavulin

Bowmore

Port Charlotte

Octomore

FROM JAPAN

Hakushu (especially Hakushu Heavily Peated)

Nikka Black

Nikka White

AGE IS JUST A NUMBER, AND OTHER FINAL THOUGHTS ABOUT SCOTCH

It's silly to boast about the age of the Scotch you drink, no matter how tied together age and prestige may be in the world of whiskey. It's probably always the case that when a distiller or blender offers a twelve-year-old and an eighteen-year-old Scotch, the latter is more expensive. But that doesn't mean it's necessarily better, and especially in the case of heavily peated whiskies, younger ones can be lively and rambunctious in ways that fade out as the whisky is aged longer. Glenfiddich is sublime at fifty; Laphroaig peaks at a youthful eighteen.

Another thing to know about age: If there's a number on the label, known as an "age statement," it reflects the minimum age of the whisky in the bottle, though there may be a small amount that's older (the age and quantity thereof is often a secret, or at least it's coyly guarded knowledge). For example, all of the liquid that has gone into a twelve-year-old whisky is at least a dozen years old, and some of it may be much older—decades older, possibly, because really old whisky is often added to younger stuff to give the batch a certain depth of flavor. Once the whisky is bottled, the aging stops. So the bottle of twelve-year-old Scotch that your uncle bought in 1985 is still considered twelve years old, no matter what he may tell the fellas down at the Legion. Only aging in wood counts—not glass—because oak is what gives whisky its flavor.

Don't get wrapped up in single malt status either. There are plenty of blended whiskies that carry enough elegance (and cost) to put them up in the special-occasion category alongside single malts. I'm thinking of Ballantine's 17, the higher colors on the Johnnie Walker totem pole (Gold, Platinum, Blue), and a number of the Compass Box brands, such as light-as-a-soufflé Asyla or the deep and spicy Oak Cross.

JAPANESE WHISKY

Japanese whiskies now win major awards with regularity, yet many in the West don't even know they exist. Or they've seen *Lost in Translation* and didn't realize that the whisky Bill Murray's character is shilling—Suntory's Hibiki 17—is one of the most sublime blended whiskies you can try. Its big sister Hibiki 21 has won so many tasting medals that its Web page is decked out like the uniform of a North Korean general.

Thanks to Shinjiro Torii and Masataka Taketsuru, distilling pioneers of the early to middle twentieth century, the whiskies of

Japan are a sort of homage to the techniques and styles of Scotland. It's a deft imitation. Even an experienced whisky hand might mistake a Yamazaki for a sherried Speyside single malt, or a Hakushu for an Islay. As in Canada, vertical integration in the whisky-making sector means Japan's distilleries often make several quite different-tasting "base whiskies" and then blend them together in various combinations to make different products. The system allows a relatively small number of distilleries to put a wide spectrum of flavors out on the market. You can visit a whiskey bar in Tokyo that offers two hundred Japanese whiskies, but they all came out of the same ten or twelve buildings.

And, yes, the overall quality of Japanese single malt has indeed matched that of Scotland, a fact that I have even heard some in the Scottish whisky industry acknowledge and admire. Others can't get past the influence of Japanese mizunara oak in that country's whisky production; the wood lends some whiskies an exuberant fruitiness and spice. Either way, I've mentally conflated the two categories, and keep Scotch and Japanese whisky together on the same shelf. Drink Japanese whisky the same way you would Scotch—with a splash of water, reserving the lighter ones for before dinner and the oilier, sherry-influenced, or peatier ones for dessert. Another way to enjoy blended Japanese whisky is to drown it in ice and water; the style is called "mizuwari" and it's supposed to make whisky palatable to drink with food or suitable for a sweltering Japanese summer's day.

IRISH WHISKEY: ONE SMOOTH CUSTOMER

Ninety percent I'll spend on good times, women, and Irish whiskey. The other ten percent I'll probably waste.

—TUG McGRAW,
RETIRED BASEBALL RELIEF PITCHER

A GLASS OF BUSHMILLS BLACK BUSH is a miraculous thing: It starts with a whiff of bourbon, all vanilla and sweet caramel. Then the nuance of the spirit starts to come out: cream, and menthol—these are not necessarily notes that the whiskey picked up from a bourbon cask; these are not imported flavors, but the whiskey's essential Irishness. As many an old barley wolfhound will tell you, this is a whiskey that won't set you back much, and yet I defy anyone to come up with a fault in it.

And don't even ask me to describe Yellow Spot. Look, there's a tear in my eye.

Irish whiskey is the original whiskey and yet these days the most overlooked, enjoying little of the prestige of Scotch or the popularity of bourbon, Tennessee whiskey, and Canadian whisky. The eclipsing of Irish whiskey is an injustice that cannot stand, and I predict that it won't.

While there is of course variation from one Irish whiskey to another, the overall picture is that this is the Goldilocks porridge of whiskey: not too light, as Canadian can be for some people; not too expensive (and bewildering), like Japanese and Scotch can be; and without the big flavor flourishes of bourbon. Irish whiskey is generally pretty calm and smooth, as friendly as the island it comes from. (Irish whiskey can come from either side of the border, the Republic of Ireland or Northern Ireland. If that matters to you— well, it shouldn't.)

Irish whiskey may be easy drinking, but in another sense it's not easy at all. This is whiskey that the advanced class can enjoy just as easily as beginners. It's subtle: The Irish themselves may talk your ear off but their whiskey tends not to bat you over the head with what it wants to say. You have to slow down and listen carefully. Of course that's also true of Japanese whisky and most Scotch from the mainland (as opposed to the islands), but I'll share this advice underlined twice when it comes to Irish whiskey: The distracted will miss a thing or two on the first go around, as will beginners. Anyone will, really. So if you enjoy an Irish whiskey, remember the name of the brand. Try it again at regular intervals to see if there's a new facet you haven't noticed before. I suppose I've just given you an excuse to drink it again. You're welcome.

Before we move on, here are the three (and a half) categories to keep in mind when exploring Irish whiskey.

BLENDS

As with blended Scotches and Japanese whisky, blended Irish whiskeys are the big sellers by volume and tend to be relatively affordable (but not always), and this is not a bad thing. In the case of Irish whiskey, blends dominate the picture especially heavily, with single malts relatively rare in day-to-day life and bars that aren't specialist whiskey joints or quality Irish pubs. (Incidentally, if you enter an Irish pub that carries only blended Irish whiskeys and no single malts or single pot stills, pivot on your heel and walk straight back out.) Great examples of blends: Powers Gold Label, Bushmills Black Bush.

SINGLE MALTS

Once again Scotch makes an apt analogy: As in Scotland, an Irish single malt is the product of a single distillery, made exclusively from malted (kiln-toasted) barley, not cut with any simple grain whiskey. They command a higher-than-average price. You're paying for extra complexity and softness of approach. Examples to try: Bushmill's single malts (various ages), Jameson 12, Connemara (funky and oily, it's the only peated Irish whiskey), Tyrconnell, and Locke's (my personal favorite).

PURE POT STILL

Like single malt whiskey, pure pot still is made at a single distillery, but in this case it's made from a mixed mash of malted and unmalted barley. The result is a flavorful style of whiskey that has really captured the interest of the world's booze writers in recent years, many of whom are developing calluses on their typing fingers trying to spread the word. Some beautiful examples: the round and robust Redbreast and Green Spot and its twelve-year-old elder sibling, Yellow Spot, which are dizzyingly complex whiskeys that balance their vanilla-laden, toasty sweetness with fresh herbal and spicy aromatics.

WRITERS TEARS

A category unto itself to the best of my knowledge, Writers Tears is labeled as a "pot still Irish whiskey" (no mention of "pure") and is a mixture of single malt and pure pot still whiskeys. In other words, it's a combination of the previous two categories. Writers Tears—note no apostrophe; they must have been trying to get under the skins of writers (and especially editors) just a little—is a grippingly multifaceted whiskey, with molasses–plum sauce sweetness and sweet citrus and bourbon-like grain and dry spice. If this writer is crying, they're tears of joy.

BOURBON AND OTHER WHISKEYS OF NORTH AMERICA

Almost none of the stories or dates on bourbon bottles are true, but asking, "Is the story true?" sort of misses the point. Ask instead, "Is it good?" . . . The bourbon inside the bottle usually is.

—REID MITENBULER, IN *BOURBON EMPIRE: THE PAST AND FUTURE OF AMERICA'S WHISKEY*

NORTH AMERICAN WHISKEY retains more of the air of toughness, an outlaw spirit, than the other major kinds of whiskey. That makes a certain amount of sense: The chill of Prohibition hangs over the continent still—still!—in the form of restrictive liquor laws and even dry counties. Alcohol remains infused with menace in the North American psyche, and other than absinthe, nothing quite says badass like a glass of brown liquor. The distillers even use product placement to ensure their whiskeys fill the background in cowboy and biker and gangster stories, to help burnish the legend.

OTHER THAN ABSINTHE, NOTHING QUITE SAYS BADASS LIKE A GLASS OF BROWN LIQUOR

Yet for all the leather-and-bullets associations, most of the whiskeys of the United States and Canada are carefully made craft products, and they continue to improve each year. Competition for the whiskey lover's dollar (not to mention pound, yuan, and ruble) is helping master distillers argue to their corporate bosses that they should be allowed to make the highly refined special editions they had always dreamt of, and I happen to know find joy in the opportunity to create something great. No longer just bland stuff to mix with soft drinks, North American whiskey deserves to be spoken of in the same breath as Scotch. Or at least the loftier portion of it does.

BOURBON

The paradox of bourbon is that it's often treated as the beginner whiskey even as it packs more of a "whoa there!" kick than the other kinds. Bourbon is the most flavorful of whiskeys. It is whiskey written in Magic Marker compared with Scotch's quill pen and Irish whiskey's pastel tones. Though it speaks simply, it has a lot to say: Bourbon is like a big fella who moves and expresses himself with surprising grace, like a baritone opera singer or sumo wrestler.

Like a few other *B*s (barbecue, blues, and baseball), bourbon is one of those American inventions that pretend they're the embodiment of folksy simplicity while they actually represent a carefully honed and cherished cultural tradition. Let us be clear, however, that quality bourbon is a tradition that mostly emerged in the twentieth century, no matter what sort of pseudohistoric cloak it's wrapped in. As whiskey writer Dave Broom observes: "The tales that swirl around bourbon are drawn from family histories, half-truths and suppositions." Indeed, we must always remember that the stories distillers tell about themselves are usually sprinkled with a healthy layer of exaggeration, but it doesn't really detract from the product.

A few simple truths: To be called bourbon, the whiskey must be made in the United States, but not—contrary to what I hear drunkenly repeated here and there—in Bourbon County or even in the state of Kentucky. (Fun fact: There's a persuasive theory that says bourbon is named for Bourbon Street in New Orleans, where it was popularized, and not Bourbon County anyway.) You can make bourbon in Yankee-infested locales like New York, and people do—be sure to try Hudson Baby Bourbon if you can.

Before the 1940s, the word *bourbon* could be used to describe a lot of things. Popularity led to codification: Regulations were created to guarantee, among other things, that 51 percent of the "mash"—which is what the fermented grain liquid is called in American distilling—must be corn (that is, maize), and that bourbon must be aged for two years. "Straight bourbon" must be four years old before bottling.

Finally, to make sure every sip of bourbon packs the expected eye-watering intensity, bourbon makers must use new, freshly charred American white oak barrels every time. This regulation forces the bourbon industry to sell off its barrels after a single use. They mostly end up in other whiskey-producing countries (Ireland, Canada, Japan, and Scotland), as well as in Mexico, where they're used to age tequila and mezcal. I'll connect the dots for you: That means that most whiskey is bourbon-flavored regardless of where it comes from, and so is a great deal of tequila.

Bourbon truly shed its homey modesty in the 1980s and 1990s when Booker Noe at the Jim Beam distillery got the idea to start producing high-end editions like Knob Creek, and others followed his lead. Single-barrel bourbons are often especially prized because they are, as the name implies, drawn and bottled from one barrel at a time. The usual practice in whiskey making is to blend the contents of different barrels to try to maintain a consistent flavor. Single-barrel bourbons like Booker's (named for Booker Noe) vary from batch to batch, and you can imagine how that phenomenon would excite a certain kind of fanboy or fangirl collecting instinct.

Bourbons don't differ as much from one brand to another as some other whiskey categories, but there are certain choices that distillers make that lead to appreciable differences. To get a sense of the diversity of bourbon, such as it is, try brands from across the following categories.

Wheated bourbons:

Bourbons with a high wheat content end up relatively sweet and mellow, making them a terrific place to begin. Maker's Mark original is the classic example, with its cherry and cream flavors. If you enjoy that, try Bernheim and W.L. Weller—as well as Van Winkle or Jefferson's bourbons, if you can find them.

High rye content:

Rye grain lends a sour and peppery-prickly flavor to whiskey, as well as some interesting fragrant and grape-like aromas. Taste Bulleit and Basil Hayden's. Then try Four Roses Small Batch, if it's available where you live.

Extra oaky:

All bourbon is oaky in the sense that it contains a hefty amount of the natural caramels, vanillin, and other compounds that whiskey absorbs from wood. But some bourbons are even woodier than others, often because they've simply spent more hot summers absorbing the goodness through the pores of the wood. These bourbons can taste like licking an antique desk, and it's wonderful. I'm quite fond of Woodford Reserve, Booker's, and Elijah Craig. Other wood lovers swear by Knob Creek, but I'm not sold.

Lovely all-arounders:

I couldn't personally slot Baker's or Blanton's neatly into any of the above categories if I tried, but they're worth mentioning and having. So is Jim Beam Black, which is my go-to "cheap" bourbon for cocktails, and it's also perfectly sippable in a pinch.

TENNESSEE WHISKEY

Jack Daniel's is often mistaken for bourbon; that's a forgivable offense, considering that the main difference is that Tennessee whiskey is smoothed out a little by filtration through maple charcoal in what's called "the Lincoln County process," which you'll want to take note of if you're looking for a name for your country-rock cover band. Otherwise it's identical to bourbon.

Jack probably accounts for 99 percent of the Tennessee whiskey sold in the world. Americans might react with bemusement to see just how incredibly popular it is in Britain and Australia. Jack Daniel's is one of the gentlest of American whiskeys, a real pussycat. Too soft for me. When I see how bikers and other supposed tough guys make soft old Jack Daniel's part of their rough-and-tumble personas, I laugh—not to their faces, obviously.

Meanwhile, a Tennessee whiskey called Dickel No. 12 that was formerly available only in the States can at last be found in some other countries. It has won my heart and captured my loyalty in this category thanks to an exquisite balance between fruity vanilla sweetness (mmm, grapes), creamy texture, and a bit of smoky bite.

As with bourbon, Tennessee whiskey barrels can't be reused to make more Tennessee whiskey and are sold onward for new purposes. Tabasco sauce is aged in ex–Jack Daniel's barrels, as are some tequilas.

RYE WHISKEY

Bourbon somehow feels old-fashioned, but its popularity isn't. If anything, bourbon is peaking in the 2010s. You don't see a lot of mention of the stuff in books published before Prohibition. So what kinds of whiskeys were Americans drinking before that? Plenty was simple blended American whiskey (which is mostly obscure these days and rarely available outside the United States; think Seagram's 7 Crown). And people drank rye.

Rye whiskey is delicious. Not in a forgiving way, mind you: Rye is a dry, sour, earthy, and austere form of whiskey. People often find hints of flavors like pepper and pickle juice within, and these are things they note with approval. In fairness I should note that I often encounter hints of concord grape and other flashes of sweetness, so it's not all sandpaper to the palate.

Rediscovered and poured with great enthusiasm since about 2007, rye has exploded. To cope with the burgeoning demand, many distillers—from spunky start-ups to established power-houses—have turned to one company, MGP Ingredients, and its distillery in Lawrenceburg, Indiana, to meet the unexpected need. MGP reportedly supplies the whiskey for a number of brands that bottle it under their own names, including Bulleit, High West, George Dickel, and Templeton. Online commentators may imply that the practice of buying alcohol in bulk and marketing it as a craft product is shady, but the whiskey is tasty (flowers and white pepper), so I don't really mind. I never believe the branding narrative anyway, and neither should you.

CANADIAN WHISKY

Look around the bars of New York or San Francisco or maybe even London and you might spot the silky-smooth-yet-spicy whiskies of my home country popping their polite little Canadian heads out of their foxholes. They're saying hello after a long spell in the doldrums of snobbish disfavor. Even in Canada, the native variety of whisky couldn't get much respect between roughly the years of 1980 to 2010. As journalist Kevin Chong wrote in *The Walrus*, Canada's smarty-pants equivalent to *The Atlantic* or *Harper's*: "Lacklustre marketing, misinformation, and reflexive feelings of national inferiority [kept] the greater drinking populace from sipping it alongside the finest bourbons and scotches."

For decades, Canadian whisky was popular even if seldom respected. The whiskey elitists might have frowned on its easy-drinking nature, but in Canada and the United States (and to a lesser extent in Japan and South Korea), Canadian whisky has consistently been downed in vast quantities as an affordable mixing spirit.

On the rare occasions when Americans ponder Canadian whisky as anything more than something to layer underneath a solid glug of cola, they think of it as the whiskey of the Prohibition era—a northern lifeline of professionally made spirit supplied at a time when the neighbo(u)rs to the south really needed it. Some will recall a tide of Canadian whisky washing up at the feet of Steve Buscemi in the opening sequence of HBO's now-concluded *Boardwalk Empire*, a recent example of North American whiskey mythmaking.

All right, so what is Canadian whisky? It bears some similarity to Irish whiskey in terms of distillation technique. Canadian whisky has a restrained, buttoned-down smoothness when compared with the high-intensity moxie of bourbon or Scotch. The grain employed is similar to the mix we find in bourbon—corn, barley, and rye; wheat and triticale are occasionally used.

In Canadian whisky's case, the grains aren't mixed together before fermentation, as they are in the States; they're distilled into separate whiskies, which, when ready, are blended to create different products. This approach allows for a variety of different brands to be produced under a single roof, and it's reminiscent of how the whisky industry works in Japan.

I tend to think of Canadian whisky as divisible into two camps. First, you have the traditional old softies that lean heavily on the sweetness of corn and barley. Most of the planet has access to examples of these—namely, Canadian Club Premium and Crown

Royal Deluxe, two easy-drinking, widely popular products that epitomize old-fashioned Canadian whisky: smooth and creamy with lots of vanilla and dark fruit (cherry), finishing with spice that's merely a pleasant tickle compared to bourbon. These are versatile whiskeys, mixable into cocktails but also perfectly sippable with water. There are higher-end examples of this style for high rollers, too: the elegant Crown Royal Extra Rare, for example.

Then you have the rye-heavy and all-rye Canadian whiskeys. In Canada, you encounter a lot of people who would rather drink the relatively gritty Alberta Premium or Wiser's Deluxe (or, at the high end, Wiser's Legacy) than the world-famous CC or Crown Royal. The spicier, rye-heavy style of Canadian whisky is not always easy stuff to find outside Canada, but certain brands are being marketed abroad these days. Take Alberta Premium Dark Horse, which the world's leading expert on Canadian whisky, Davin de Kergommeaux, described as "Slate, charcoal, bourbon-like vanilla, sweet pickles, dark fruits, sweet and herbal flowers, hot pepper, sweet ginger and crispy clean oak. An extraordinary symphony of rye." Masterson's is a posh sibling to Dark Horse and worth the high price tag. Or there's my personal favorite, Lot No. 40. Made from 100 percent rye grain and distilled in a copper pot still, it explodes with fruit and spice. I'm biased as a proud Canadian, but I don't believe there's a better all-around rye for cocktails.

The tendency is for Canadian rye-heavy whiskeys to be fruitier and more peppery and less influenced by oak than American rye. But when a recipe calls for rye, go ahead and use either one. The results will differ but should offer a nice, sweet, tasty burn either way.

THE OLD FASHIONED, MANHATTAN, AND OTHER WHISKEY COCKTAILS

> The latest drink of the habitués of Madison Square [is] called an "old-fashioned cocktail. . . . Very soothing and grateful to the palate is this decoction."
>
> —*THE SUN* (NEW YORK), JUNE 1890

JUST AS *HOMO SAPIENS* replaced *Homo erectus* and the Romance languages evolved from Latin, the old fashioned is a direct descendant of the original cocktail, which first pops up by name in early-nineteenth-century New York State—though its origins may stretch back further than that. (And I'm not going to get into the origins of cocktails or the word *cocktail*, except to say that they're complicated, and many of the stories you encounter are wrong.)

In those days the cocktail was a simple but satisfying mixture of spirits, water, bitters, and sugar. Later iterations, from the Manhattan to the mojito, hadn't been created yet. Cocktails were mainly a means to make spirits easier to get down your throat. Meanwhile, spirits and bitters were thought of as medicinal. You might start your morning with a cocktail because you thought it would kick your hangover.

The base was often brandy, not whiskey. (American whiskey was probably pretty awful in the early nineteenth century, no matter how much you masked it with sugar and bitters.) Brandy plus the other ingredients made a "brandy cocktail." Gin (by which the fellas meant genever) made a gin cocktail, and so on.

Eventually, ice appeared, and this novelty improved the cocktail tremendously. Whiskey became more refined as the century unfolded. A twist of citrus peel did wonders for the cocktail as well. These developments put the cocktail well on its evolutionary path toward becoming the modern-day old fashioned.

Where did the name come from? As new kinds of cocktails appeared on the scene around the 1860s and 1870s—Manhattans, martinis, and the like, which contained fortified wine and other novel ingredients—the whiskey cocktail had to be defined against its upstart rivals. I imagine it happening quite organically: A gentleman would lean over the bar and ask for an "old-fashioned whiskey cocktail," and he might suggest he didn't want any newfangled ingredients, like them yoo-ro-pean wines, mucking it up.

In those days (and indeed in ours), an old fashioned might still be made from brandy or another spirit that wasn't bourbon. But I've included it in the chapter for whiskey cocktails because since Prohibition, the old fashioned has usually been made with whiskey, especially bourbon. (At home I often use rye as opposed to bourbon, and you haven't really tried all the possibilities till you've had an old fashioned made with armagnac.)

As a modern bourbon drink, the old fashioned is the common denominator for the craft cocktail bar: Try to show me a place that doesn't serve one. During its second, twenty-first-century, heyday, the old fashioned has also been fairly explicitly affirmed as a totem of virility. It's a go-to for Don Draper in the television series *Mad Men*, as well as for Ryan Gosling's character in *Crazy, Stupid, Love* (it's the drink he makes when seducing Emma Stone. It works). These characters are playboys, Don Juans. I hope this trend in the depiction of old fashioneds will not put off women from trying one.

An old fashioned is sweet and powerful and nuanced. People

have been drinking them for two centuries and continue to revel in their simple perfection. You will encounter many variations of the old fashioned; many will be worth trying, but you'll probably just end up going back to plain old bourbon and rye, maybe cognac and rum on occasion. Whatever the spirit, I don't know any serious cocktail fans who ever really get tired of old fashioneds. It is a curious fact that the old fashioned never actually gets old.

IT IS A CURIOUS FACT THAT THE OLD FASHIONED NEVER ACTUALLY GETS OLD.

Making them for oneself is enjoyable as well; it's a little ritual of a procedure, like so:

Old Fashioned

- Standard sugar cube, or substitute 1 teaspoon rich simple syrup
- 2 dashes Angostura bitters (or another brand that makes an herbally complex substitute, such as Bitter Truth Aromatic Bitters or Fee Brothers Whiskey Barrel-Aged Bitters)
- 2 ounces quality bourbon (or other spirit, such as rye)
- Twist of orange peel, for garnish

1. Place the sugar cube in the bottom of a mixing glass and douse it with the bitters and about a teaspoon of water.

2. Smoosh the sugar cube and stir it around until it turns into a sort of paste. A barspoon with a blunt end specifically for this purpose is shown, but you can just use any spoon, or a muddler.

3. Add the bourbon, fill the mixing glass most of the way up with ice, and stir.

4. Strain into a rocks glass with ice, ideally one big cube (using a two-inch-by-two-inch ice cube mold). Use your julep strainer if you have one.

5. Now we need our orange peel garnish. (We use this procedure in a lot of cocktails, including the martini with a lemon twist, so knowing how to do this is an everyday cocktail skill.) Start by using your vegetable peeler to make a wide ribbon of orange peel—wide, but not deep: Avoid taking very much of the white pith below the surface, which tastes bitter. You can trim the peel into a perfect rectangle if you're in a fussy sort of mood, or leave it as it is.

6. Squeeze the orange peel above the surface of the drink. The aim is to flavor your old fashioned with the essential oils that are locked inside; in bright enough lighting, you can see a little spray of oil when you perform this step. Some people like to hold a match in the path of the stream to create a little fire show; search YouTube and watch how professional bartenders safely perform this trick. Whether or not you flame the peel, drop it into the old fashioned and serve.

THE MANHATTAN

Remember that time Bart Simpson stumbled into Springfield's Legitimate Businessman's Social Club and landed a job as a bartender to Fat Tony and his mafioso cronies? Bart somehow demonstrates a knack for the rye-and-vermouth mixture, endearing him to the crooks. I wish he'd give lessons to some less ambitious bartenders around North America. To echo the words of Fat Tony's rival, who receives an inferior rendition after Bart is forced to quit: "What have I done to deserve this flat and flavorless Manhattan?"

Indeed, what did we do? When I first started drinking cocktails in bars, circa 1998, Manhattans—at least in Toronto—were flat and flavorless indeed. They employed bourbon or mild Canadian whisky, which are too sweet for the task, instead of spicy, dry, full-bodied rye. They were probably made from vermouth that was stale from sitting on the bar after being opened. They sometimes skipped the Angostura bitters, and worse still, they would add the red syrup from the cherry jar to sweeten the mixture. Bartenders counted a lazy circular agitation of a cocktail shaker as "stirring," or would shake it. I was even taught these procedures in bartending school: All of it was unintentional blasphemy.

A made-to-specifications Manhattan consists of rye, sweet vermouth, and bitters—Angostura, according to the canon—garnished with a maraschino cherry. You stir it properly, with a barspoon.

The ingredients matter: This is a three-legged stool, and the whole thing falls over if you skimp on any part of the triad. Toronto restaurateur Jen Agg made an entire city fall in love with Manhattans again by crafting them much as they'd been prepared up to the early twentieth century: with quality rye (she uses Alberta-made whisky, but American rye, such as Sazerac or Rittenhouse, would work, too), Carpano Antica Formula vermouth, house-made bitters, and house-made cherries, tiny and so dark purple they're almost black—a far cry from the kind at the grocery store.

A balanced Manhattan will feature the spice of the bitters and the vermouth, balanced against the kick of the rye, neither facet dominating. Compared with an old fashioned, a Manhattan is less sweet and thinner and less silky in texture because there's no added sugar.

Manhattan

- 2 ounces rye whiskey (not bourbon!)
- 1 ounce sweet vermouth (preferably Carpano classico or Carpano Antica Formula)
- 2 dashes Angostura bitters
- 1 quality brandied cherry (such as Luxardo brand), for garnish

Add the rye, vermouth, and bitters to a cocktail shaker with ice and stir until nice and cold. Strain into a chilled cocktail glass or over one large ice cube in a rocks glass (I prefer the former). Garnish with a cherry.

THE SAZERAC

It seems almost obligatory for people to refer to the well-known bartender Paul Gustings as "crusty" or "cranky," but I found him anything but when I first tracked him down at Tujague's restaurant in New Orleans. It was a Friday late afternoon and I had the burly old Dutch American to myself for an hour or so while the after-work crowd trickled in: laborers in overalls, a chatty blond state bureaucrat with a foul mouth and a white pencil skirt suit, and of course tourists of all descriptions. There aren't many chairs at Tujague's, and this decorating choice did its usual trick of getting people from all walks of life chatting, which we did as the golden hour light spilled in sideways through the front door and onto the checkered floor.

Gustings (who now works at a different joint; Google him to

keep track) was in a terrific mood. Smiling, even. So I asked him to show me the correct way to make a sazerac, and he did.

Other cocktails originate in New Orleans: the hurricane, the Ramos gin fizz, and the vieux carré, for example. But no cocktail is closer to NOLA's heart than the sazerac, an old fashioned with a couple of Creole twists. I revisit the warming memory of that late afternoon—and Gustings's recipe—every time I enjoy a sazerac.

Incidentally, this is thought of as a rye cocktail and probably has been one since the 1930s. But cognac was the original spirit when the sazerac was conceived in the nineteenth century, and some still prefer it. I usually split the difference and use an ounce each of cognac and rye.

Sazerac

- About 1 teaspoon absinthe or Herbsaint (a Louisiana anise liquor)
- 1 sugar cube
- 1 dash Angostura bitters
- 3–5 dashes Peychaud's bitters (a lot, I know)
- 2 ounces rye whiskey (or cognac, or a combination thereof)
- 1 lemon wedge

1. Chill a rocks/old fashioned glass (for example, by sticking it in the freezer). Once it's cold, add the absinthe, swirl the glass around to coat the inside with the spirit, and discard the excess.

2. In a separate mixing glass, add the sugar cube, a splash of water, and the bitters. Muddle until the sugar is mostly dissolved.

3. Add a scoop of ice and the rye into the mixing glass, and stir gently for at least 60 seconds, preferably 90.

4. Strain into the prepared glass. *Do not add ice.* Squeeze a piece of lemon over the glass and garnish with the lemon only if the guest/customer so desires.

THE BOULEVARDIER

I reserve the right to change my mind, but when asked about my favorite cocktail, I have often named the boulevardier. It's sort of a cross between an old fashioned and a Manhattan, with Campari on the scene to impart some European-style bitterness.

The boulevardier (bool-uh-vard-YAY) was the invention of one Erskine Gwynne, a member of the Vanderbilt family who had a short and tragic life. He died in 1948 a little under fifty years old, after ten years of paralysis following a car accident that also killed his cousin. In happier times, Gwynne had been a regular at Harry's New York Bar, an American hangout in 1920s Paris (it should have appeared in Woody Allen's *Midnight in Paris*), which recorded his preferred order—a mixture of equal parts bourbon, Campari, and vermouth—in its cocktail books for posterity. Owner Harry McElhone named the drink after Gwynne's magazine; *boulevardier* means something like "man about town."

As is the usual practice in our time, I bump up the amount of bourbon in my boulevardiers from Gwynne's too-light single ounce.

Boulevardier

- 1–1½ ounces bourbon
- 1 ounce Campari
- 1 ounce sweet vermouth
- Twist of orange peel, for garnish

Stir the bourbon, Campari, and vermouth with ice in a mixing glass until nice and cold. Strain into a chilled cocktail glass or over one large piece of ice in a rocks glass. Squeeze the orange peel to spray the essential oils onto the surface of the drink, and drop it into the drink.

MORE WHISKEY COCKTAILS

Whiskey Sour

Not my favorite, but I'll share a recipe because it's so popular and others find it useful. The odd dive bar outdoes itself by making one that's surprisingly drinkable.

- 2 ounces cheap bourbon
- Sugar, to taste—start with 1 teaspoon or so and go from there
- Juice of ½ lemon
- Maraschino cherry, for garnish

Add the bourbon, sugar, and lemon juice to a cocktail shaker filled with ice and shake well. Some add a little float of Bordeaux (claret) wine to the top, but most feel that a cherry makes a sufficient garnish.

Brainstorm

A bit drier than some of the other whiskey cocktails, and a handy one to keep in your back pocket.

- 1½ ounces rye whiskey
- ½ ounce dry vermouth
- ½ ounce Bénédictine
- Twist of orange peel, for garnish

Fill a mixing glass two-thirds of the way up with ice. Add the rye, vermouth, and Bénédictine, and stir until very cold. Squeeze the orange peel to spray the essential oils onto the surface of the drink; then float the peel on top, and serve.

RUM AND RUM COCKTAILS

I am sure there is some elixir of life in ration rum. . . . I am
convinced there is something very extraordinary about it. I
have seen European soldiers worship liquor, give their lives
for it, and often lose their lives trying to get it.

—SITA RAM, EARLY-NINETEENTH-CENTURY
BENGAL ARMY OFFICER

ONE RUM CAN BE AS DIFFERENT from an-
other as a cold mountain stream is from a warm, tur-
quoise tropical lagoon. Because it's made in a multitude
of ways in different places, rum spans the range from water-clear
and sweetly aromatic white rum (take Bacardi Superior, for example) to rum that's as black as the alien depths of an oceanic trench
(Cruzan Black Strap, from the U.S. Virgin Islands) to rums of all
hues that are as funky as a Parliament bass line (groove to the deep
gold-colored Smith & Cross from Jamaica, for example).

Saying you don't like rum is a little like saying you don't like
cake: Extensive exploration may confirm the suspicion, but you'd
want to try a few different kinds before making such a sweeping
declaration.

What unites the vast, multicolored, and multicultural rum
family is this: They're all made from molasses, the sticky brown
goo left over after sugarcane is processed and the more highly val-
ued crystalline white sugar is extracted. Molasses is said to exhibit
terroir, taking on some of the essence of the places where the sugarcane was grown. That might account for at least some of the eye-
opening differences between, say, clean-tasting Cuban or Puerto

Rican rum versus warm, sugary demerara rum from Guyana. Who knows.

At this point it's difficult not to dwell for a moment on something a great deal more consequential: rum's difficult history, rooted in the plantation economies of the Caribbean and surrounding areas. Long story short: no slavery, no rum. I can't do the topic any justice here, so I'll just suggest that further delving into the topic makes for sobering and enlightening reading.

Today, thanks to its associations with sunny holiday destinations, rum is usually thought of as a happy fun-time beverage. Yet it can be brooding and deep, particularly unmixed. A snifter of a refined aged rum (Zacapa, El Dorado, Plantation, or the older rums from Mount Gay, Appleton Estate, or Havana Club) has been suggested as "the new Scotch" or "the new cognac." It's not. Even the finest rums have too many rubbery flavors and hard edges to qualify as the equal of those other spirits. But you can also relish flavors and aromas like vanilla, orange, and brown sugar, together with interesting floral notes. It all makes rum an interesting change of pace for the habitual drinker of a postprandial whiskey or brandy. I also think drinking a glass of rum neat—which is not a common practice outside the Caribbean, no matter how many men's blogs say it's the big new thing—will have the effect of heightening your allure. A person who drinks straight rum is not to be messed with.

A tip, meanwhile: Any rum fine enough to sip is a rum that will make a beautiful old fashioned.

If it's sunnier times you're after, a daiquiri or a mojito will do. A tiki drink, meanwhile, elevates the party feeling to giddy altitudes, but beware the crash: Rum is sweetish, and its alcoholic jab is easily concealed by its traditional companions, citrus juice and sugar. Many rum recipes contain a heavier glug of spirit than you (or your guests) might have assumed.

Standard Daiquiri

At a typical bar, or an all-inclusive resort, or at one of those drive-thru cocktail windows in Louisiana, a "daiquiri" is a slushy beverage full of artificial colors and flavors. I'm not saying you can't enjoy such a thing when the occasion is right for a bit of silliness. But you should also do yourself a favor and try a daiquiri as it was originally conceived: hand shaken (no blender), no slush, and with real, fresh juice.

- Generous 2 ounces white (or amber) rum
- ½ ounce simple syrup
- Juice of ½ lime
- Lime wedge or wheel, for garnish

Add the rum and simple syrup to a cocktail shaker, then squeeze half a lime directly in after them (it's wise to do the squeezing over the shaker so that the essential oils in the lime peel make their way into the drink, too). Add ice, seal the shaker, and shake well. Strain into a chilled cocktail glass, and garnish with the wedge or float a really thin lime wheel on top. (Tip: Try substituting maraschino liqueur for the simple syrup.)

Mojito

The secret to a great mojito, according to a scene in Steven Soder-bergh's four-hour film Che, is to gently squish the mint leaves, not muddling them so hard that they rip. This is a tip that Fidel Castro gives someone at a party. I agree with his cocktail advice if not his politics.

Mojitos may be delicious—Havana's contribution to refreshing drinking, and a laudable one—but bartenders hate them because they involve a lot of effort. You'll hate mojitos, too, if you offer to make them for a party. Be stingy: Keep mojitos to yourself—unless someone else is doing the muddling.

- 2 teaspoons granulated sugar
- Juice of ½ lime
- 3 healthy-looking mint sprigs
- 1½ ounces rum (ideally Havana Club Añejo 3 Años)
- Club soda

1. To a highball glass, add the sugar, a tiny initial spray of lime juice, and two mint sprigs. I point the leaves downward so that they're better exposed to muddling.

2. Remember El Jefe's advice: Muddle gently.

3. Add ice cubes and the rest of the lime juice. Stir well.

4. Add the rum, and stir well again.

5. Fill the glass with club soda. Stir again, gently. Garnish with the remaining mint sprig (consider reserving the prettiest one for this purpose).

Papa Doble

Also known as a "Hemingway daiquiri," this variation on the theme is named after the man who is supposed to have invented it. The (otherwise pretty boring) novel Islands in the Stream *gives us an inkling of how he enjoyed them: "The great ones that Constante made had no taste of alcohol and felt, as you drank them, the way downhill glacier skiing feels running through powder snow and, after the sixth and eighth, felt like downhill glacier skiing feels when you are running unroped." Don't drink eight of them, or even six. That sliding downhill sensation will be you hitting the floor.*

- 2 ounces good white or amber rum
- ½ ounce freshly squeezed grapefruit juice
- ¾ ounce freshly squeezed lime juice
- ¼ ounce maraschino liqueur
- Lime wheel or wedge, for garnish

Add the rum, juices, and maraschino to a cocktail shaker filled halfway with ice and shake hard until the mixture is ice cold. Strain into a chilled cocktail glass. Garnish with a lime wheel or wedge.

Dark and Stormy

The one and only time I was ever invited to a regatta (#regattabrag), it was in Key West, Florida, and I spent the whole time in a slight haze thanks to the hosts' generosity with this easy, spicy, refreshing rum beverage. Just be careful: two ounces of rum per drink is not unheard of.

Gosling's Black Seal is the traditional, and some would say only, choice for the rum. It's a smooth, deep brown number redolent of molasses and cream soda that hails from Bermuda. Not only that, but Gosling's actually owns the trademark Dark 'N Stormy, incorrectly used apostrophe and all.

- 4 ounces ginger beer
- 2 ounces dark rum
- Lime wedge, for garnish

Fill a short tumbler or highball glass with ice—I like to crush it first—and pour the ginger beer up to the two-thirds mark. Then top with the dark rum. The visual effect that results is a band of brown sugar atop a pale green sea. Include a lime wedge, and encourage the squeezing thereof into the drink.

Mai Tai

Tiki bar impresario Victor "Trader Vic" Bergeron claimed ownership of the mai tai. Anyone who denied it, he said, was "a stinker." If you can track down the two specialty syrups and make a proper one, you'll see why he was so keen to take credit. Rock candy syrup can be found through specialty cocktail retailers; if you're in more of a hurry than that, use simple syrup made with 2 parts sugar to 1 part water, or the Torani brand of cane sugar syrup works fine as well. Orgeat is a nutty-sweet syrup made from almonds (try Italian specialty food stores or cocktail supply stores for that).

- Juice of ½ lime
- 1 ounce dark Jamaican rum
- 1 ounce rhum agricole (see below)
- ½ ounce Cointreau
- ¼ ounce 2:1 simple syrup, Torani Cane Syrup, or—best of all—rock candy syrup
- ¼ ounce Orgeat
- Spent lime shell and mint sprig, for garnish
- Paper umbrella, edible flower, cherry, and/or large pineapple wedge (optional but recommended)

Fill a cocktail shaker halfway with ice and squeeze the lime juice into it. Reserve spent lime shell. Add the rum, rhum agricole, Cointreau, simple syrup, and Orgeat; shake the mixture vigorously and pour into a glass or tiki drinking vessel without straining. Garnish festively.

CACHAÇA AND RHUM AGRICOLE

Cachaça and rhum agricole are both relations of rum proper, but not quite rum by definition as they're made from sugarcane juice as opposed to molasses. Cachaça (kah-SHAH-sah) is the national spirit of Brazil, while rhum agricole comes from the French-speaking Caribbean.

As with rum and tequila, these spirits start white and hot in their clear, young versions and turn amber and mellow as they're aged. Even in their older, posher renditions, neither cachaça nor rhum agricole is the easiest-drinking spirit on the shelf. Exotic, oily flavors abound, and without the warm blanket of sweetness you encounter in rum from English- and Spanish-speaking regions. Drinking cachaça or rhum agricole straight? You'll require a leather esophagus for that, or else plenty of experience.

You can attenuate them as per the following instructions. The caipirinha is Brazil's unofficial national cocktail, while the ti' punch is Martinique's after-dinner tipple.

Caipirinha

I've set up a make-your-own caipirinha station at a party at my place a couple of times. It's always a hit. Anyone can make this. Just put out the instructions (I find it helps to draw a picture for each step, too).

- ½ plump lime, cut into four wedges
- 4 teaspoons sugar (raw cane sugar or turbinado)
- 2 ounces (or less) cachaça

Add the lime wedges and sugar to a rocks glass. Muddle well to extract the juice from the lime. Stir to dissolve the sugar as much as you can, but be at peace with the fact that it's going to remain grainy. Add ice, and then cachaça. Stir again.

Ti' punch

Cane syrup should be relatively easy to find if you live in the Caribbean or the southern United States—or Britain, where you'll recognize it as Lyle's Golden Syrup. Torani, the San Francisco–based maker of coffee flavorings, offers a cane syrup as well. Failing all that, just use simple syrup. Incidentally, ti is short for "petit," or "small," in French; it's the equivalent of saying "li'l" or, for the Brits, "ickle."

- 2 ounce rhum agricole
- ½ lime
- ¼–½ ounce cane syrup

Mix the rhum, lime, and syrup together right in a tumbler. (Squeeze the lime with your hand if you feel like it.) Stir to dissolve the syrup as much as possible, and add ice. I think you can get away without a garnish.

COGNAC AND OTHER
AGED BRANDIES

Claret is the liquor for boys, port for men; but he who aspires
to be a hero . . . must drink brandy.

—SAMUEL JOHNSON

B RANDY IS SOMETIMES GIVEN a pretty wide definition; some consider any spirit ultimately distilled from
fruit to be brandy. In this chapter, however, we're going to
focus on brandies that are made from wine and then aged in oak.
The best-known brandies that fit the bill are cognac and armagnac.

Between these, cognac is the most prestigious and widely recognized. France might have gone to a lot of bloody trouble to make
itself into a republic, but cognac still commands regal respect
around the world.

COGNAC

Cognac is distilled wine and must be made in the vicinity of Cognac, France. It's made from a boring white wine no one actually
seems to drink, involving grapes you've likely never heard of (such
as Ugni Blanc), yet it takes on magical properties when rested for
years in French oak.

For those who are accustomed to drinking spirits neat, cognac
is straightforward and user-friendly to drink. You just pour it into
a big glass and serve at room temperature. Prepare for your first
gulp by swirling it around in the glass, then sniff from a foot or two

away, then sniff from a shorter distance—I grant you permission to stick that nose right into the glass now. More than any other spirit, a glass of cognac is recognized as something you take slow and savor. Especially for those of us used to rougher stuff like bourbon and tequila, cognac gives off gentle aromas, sweet and fragrant. You might smell caramel, apple, apricot, and flowers of various kinds. As cognac ages, it becomes softer and more complex and nuanced—the hot finish of young brandy gives way to a sweet aroma of flowers and raisins.

Unlike its close cousin single malt whisky, you don't typically serve cognac with water. As for glasses, those big snifters are fun and they're easy to find; they even sell them at IKEA now.

Go ahead, pretend you're an aristocrat. Stare at the liquid and frown. Cognac was a must-have in the drawing rooms of the moneyed classes during the nineteenth century. The clichéd after-dinner activity for men of a certain status was to retire to a private, men-only salon for brandy, cigars, and conversation topics not appropriate for women's ears (politics? fart jokes? it's all lost in the wind now). As mentioned earlier, Cognac's heyday came to a pause when the phylloxera epidemic decimated French vines and made brandy scarce for a few decades starting in 1872. Scotch stepped in as a substitute prestige digestif, and today the two spirits are more or less rivals for the rulership of the after-dinner hour.

Though cognac is a gentle and friendly spirit compared to all the others, it will burn a little on the palate of those not accustomed to consuming spirits straight. It has more potential as a crowd-pleaser than, say, mezcal, and yet it has fallen into obscurity in many countries, notably English-speaking ones.

A minimal level of knowledge will get you through when it comes to cognac. I've got along pretty well in life simply remembering that cognacs go from VS at the cheapest to VSOP to XO at the top.

(If you see "Fine Champagne Cognac" or something similar on the label, that's a confusing reference to a section of the Cognac region that happens to be called Champagne, a fairly generic place name in France. It has nothing to do with the sparkling wine. We're on the other side of France here.)

There are cognacs that don't have a name that slots into this scheme, and you'll need to rely on reviews to tell you what's what. Courvoisier C and Hennessy Black appear to have been formulated for the club-and-cocktail market and are exuberant and flavorful enough to perform well in a mixture—but they're not sippers. Likewise, at 45% alcohol, Pierre Ferrand 1840 was born for cocktail service and performs admirably in that role, but is too hot and rough around the edges for the solemn contemplation of the fireside. On the other hand, Rémy Martin's Accord Royal is not identified as a VSOP or an XO because Rémy Martin figures it fits between the two on the quality and price hierarchy, and it does indeed possess all the softness you want in a snifter-worthy brandy.

There aren't nearly as many brands of cognac as there are of other prestige spirits. You've likely heard of the big houses, which together account for some 85 percent of the total cognac output: Courvoisier, Rémy Martin, Hennessy, and Martell. They're all reliable, but don't neglect the brands that are smaller and less likely to be shouted out at the club, such as Hine, Pierre Ferrand, and Baron Otard.

Another tip, mostly for Americans: You tend to say cognac in a unique (dare I say wrong?) way that might elicit snickers in the company of pretentious types while abroad. Don't give them the satisfaction: Say CON-yak, not CONE-yak.

No matter how you say it, cognac starts off expensive and soon reaches the ridiculous. Some brands cost as much as a compact car for a bottle, and even the everyday cognacs rival pretty pricey Scotches. Thanks to its great and growing popularity in China, French brandy is probably only going to get more expensive in the future, so get it while you can.

I get asked what the high-end cognacs are like and whether they're worth the money. They can be sublime—sorry to taunt you so—and, yes, enough so as to be worth it, if you would think nothing of spending thousands of dollars or pounds in one trip to the liquor store. I've had the good fortune to try some of the really higher-end cognacs, and L'Essence de Courvoisier and Louis XIII stand out as having been especially exquisite experiences, surprisingly lively and youthful and sweet while still beguilingly nuanced and mature and fragrant. Cognacs you can't afford are like crushes way out of your league: Best to put them out of your mind, though I admit L'Essence de Courvoisier haunts me still.

On the other end of the affordability scale, what about the cheaper brandies that are not cognac but styled as copycats: Is there anything worthwhile in them? Can we save some money here?

Not with California brandies. They use terms like VS and XO but taste to me like bubblegum—all sweetness and none of the woody complexity of the real LeCoy. Avoid them.

In my opinion the star of the cheap brandy parade is Cortel VSOP: dry crisp apple aroma, caramel on the palate, soft texture, floral notes in the finish. While it may represent good value, to suggest to a cognac lover that cognac and affordable brandy are somehow interchangeable—except perhaps if you're evaluating them as cooking ingredients—will earn you the harshest form of Gallic derision.

Sidecar

The most famous cognac cocktail is, fittingly, a French invention . . . sort of: The sidecar is supposed to have been conjured up at Harry's New York Bar, which is actually in Paris but has an American theme, and was run by a Scotsman named Harry McElhone when the sidecar appeared in the 1920s. Anyway, if you like margaritas, a sidecar makes a fine Gallic twist.

- 1½ ounces cognac
- 1 ounce Cointreau (or other orange liqueur)
- 1 ounce freshly squeezed lemon juice

Add the cognac, Cointreau, lemon juice, and ice to a shaker and shake well. Strain into a chilled cocktail glass.

COGNAC AGES

VS: "Very special" or "very superior"; aged at least two years

VSOP: "Very special old pale" or "very superior old pale"; aged at least four years

XO: "Extra old"; aged at least six years

Napoléon: Synonymous with XO

ARMAGNAC

Another French brandy that must be made in a particular region, armagnac is often grouped in with cognac, but it's made using a different kind of still and sports a distinct flavor all it's own. Those initiated into cognac may find armagnac fruitier, more robust, and even more floral. "French vodka" it certainly is not, contrary to a plotline in *The Sopranos* (importing armagnac was the get-rich-quick scheme that Tony's restaurateur pal, Artie, lost his shirt over). Armagnac can be poured and served as simply and easily as cognac and, as the Toronto restaurant Alo has discovered, makes a really smashing old fashioned. The biggest brand of armagnac is Janneau, and if you can locate Marquis de Montesquiou VSOP, you'll end up with an understanding of just how robust and fruity armagnac can be.

CALVADOS AND APPLEJACK

When the gloom and crisp air of autumn descend on my breezy lakeside hometown, part of me welcomes the annual return of the excuse to sip calvados.

Calvados is the signature spirit of the French region of Normandy, an apple brandy that's aged in oak until it emerges as a sweet spirit that's even sprightlier on its feet than cognac. While it starts off as hard cider, the distillation and aging process of calvados attenuates the apple aromas enough that if you're new to the stuff, someone might have to point them out to you. (Just as cognac has only an oblique relationship to the flavor of grapes.) But the autumnal orchard aromas are indeed present, especially in a young calvados. As calvados is aged longer it converges in flavor with cognac and whiskey; the apple aromas fade and it takes on more of the spice, vanilla, and caramel of the oak. Calvados graduates from vieux or réserve (aged two years) to VO or VSOP (aged three years) and finally to XO, Napoléon, or hors d'age (aged at least six years for any of these designations, often far longer).

While other brandies find their way into after-dinner snifters and cocktails, most calvados is destined to be poured into *le trou normand*—literally, "the Norman hole"—which refers to the practice, well known across France, of sipping a small amount of "calva" as a palate cleanser between courses. I personally feel that hard spirits deaden the palate, and I reserve them for pre- and postdinner drinks (I believe "whiskey-pairing dinners" are an abomination). However, Norman cuisine involves plenty of cream sauces and offal, and a little tongue wiper might be welcome. Anyway, it's tradition.

I'm fairly certain New Jerseyites do not typically perform *le trou normand*, but they could: Their native applejack, Laird's, is the lone major brand that survives out of a once-robust tradition of American apple brandy making.

Americans used to make apple brandy using a lazy-slash-*clever* method: "jacking." A fellow from Pennsylvania once keenly explained it to me, apparently oblivious to the dangers I discovered when I Googled it later. To jack cider, you freeze it and remove the ice. The liquid left behind is high in alcohol. Hence "applejack," which George Washington is said to have made for his troops. The trouble with jacking—or freeze distillation, as the folks down in the lab call it—is that it leaves behind unappetizing, potentially unwholesome fusel oils. It's also illegal almost everywhere. Don't do it.

Laird's applejack is made in a fashion closer to the French calvados technique. The stronger "bonded" version is superior to the regular, if you can find it. Outside the United States you probably won't be able to track down much Laird's, but microdistilleries have sprung up in apple-growing countries such as the United States, Canada, and Germany offering their own apple brandies.

I use applejack, calvados, and other apple brandies interchangeably in cocktail recipes in my house. I'm certain this will scandalize some purist bartenders of my acquaintance, but the difference isn't big enough to fuss over.

APPLE BRANDY COCKTAILS

Sharky Punch

I found this obscure but fantastic and simple little recipe in a book from the 1960s. Party guests typically ask for seconds. My twist involves a drop of Angostura bitters.

- 1½ ounces apple brandy
- ½ ounce rye whiskey
- ½ ounce simple syrup
- 1 drop Angostura bitters
- About ½ ounce club soda

Stir the apple brandy (applejack or calvados), rye, simple syrup, and bitters in a mixing glass with ice and strain into a chilled cocktail glass. Top up with the splash of soda.

Jack Rose Cocktail

A nearly forgotten simple oldie with a general similarity to the whiskey sour and daiquiri.

- 2 ounces applejack
- 1 ounce freshly squeezed lime juice
- ½ ounce grenadine

Add the applejack, lime juice, and grenadine to a cocktail shaker and fill with ice. Shake well and strain into a chilled cocktail glass.

SOME OTHER BRANDIES

Spain, Portugal, Greece, Armenia, and other countries along a similar latitude to France produce aged brandies of their own, and these call out for deeper exploration.

Slivovitz (there are other spellings), meanwhile, is aged plum brandy that comes from eastern Europe and seems to retain some popularity in the Jewish Diaspora—even the imaginary one. It was the favored drink of Meyer Landsman, the gumshoe protagonist of Michael Chabon's *The Yiddish Policeman's Union*; he "drinks to medicate himself, tuning the tubes and crystals of his moods with a crude hammer of hundred-proof plum brandy. . . . When there is crime to fight, Landsman tears around Sitka [Alaska] like a man with his pant leg caught on a rocket." Speaking of rockets, I've read comparisons between slivovitz and rocket fuel, which for the first time in my life made me feel pity for ballistic projectiles. There are evidently well-made brands, but I haven't yet had the pleasure.

HOW TO DRINK TEQUILA

In truth the problem with the taste of tequila is not just
psychological. . . . Even at its best, tequila has a dirty kind of
smell. It's freshly sweated salt . . . raw complexity of pot-
distilled alcohol; an almost sickly edge of sweetness—and
then a gulp of alcoholic heat. Perhaps that's not a great sell.
But this is feral alcohol, and that's what so good about it.

—VICTORIA MOORE, DRINKS WRITER

A THOUSAND TIMES YOU'LL HEAR someone
blaming tequila for their worst-ever night (or even worse
next morning), vowing never to touch the accursed stuff
again.

For the tequila abstainers out there, I'd like you to consider
giving Mexico's national spirit a second chance. Think back to the
night in question. Remember all the other liquids you sent down
your gullet; their fearsome quantity and variety. Remember the
choices you made.

How many mistakes were too late to take back before poor
tequila even showed up on the scene? Did tequila cause your problems, or was tequila simply the last little tiptoe over the edge?

Whatever happened to you—a hangover of Homeric anguish,
scope, and duration; a poor decision that haunts you to this day;
perhaps banishment from a small Latin American country—do you
not agree that it's a bit churlish to blame the *tequila* rather than
yourself?

Tequila's terrifying reputation in the English-speaking lands
has to do with the fact that it's consumed chiefly in bad, overly

sugary cocktails, and often appears during the witching hour, when someone makes the ill-advised suggestion of a round of shots. For most gringos, tequila is a propellant for fueling one's rocket blasts straight into Regrets Town.

All of this is amusing to Mexicans, of course, not to mention a growing number of smug gringos who know that fine tequila, sensibly imbibed, is a source of deep appreciation and pleasure.

Perhaps it's because some can harbor a lamentable tendency to underestimate the sophistication of Mexican culture, but people often look at me funny when I say I usually drink tequila straight and slowly, like cognac. But that's exactly how you should enjoy it, provided you've got yourself some 100 percent agave tequila. And if you can't find that phrase on the label, don't buy it: Otherwise what you have is a "mixto" tequila, and that's the kind you avoid.

> I USUALLY DRINK TEQUILA STRAIGHT AND SLOWLY, LIKE COGNAC.

I will concede that even at its best, tequila is not the most approachable of spirits. Some people will simply never get over that odd characteristic aroma, which is—what, exactly? I venture to say it's a strange combination of cucumber, pepper, and chocolate. When writing about Casamigos tequila (part owned by George Clooney, and it's quite good), I came up with: "cookies, grapefruit peel, menthol, Crispy Crunch bar."

Tequila is made from the fermented and distilled mush of the Weber blue agave plant, which grows in Mexico and bears a certain resemblance to aloe. Once distilled, it can be bottled without aging (and thus known as *blanco*, or silver; either way, fine in a cocktail). This is tequila at its purest, and while this is the least expensive kind of tequila, it's how many connoisseurs prefer it.

Tequila that's yellow or amber in color has been aged in ex–whiskey barrels (bourbon or Tennessee whiskey), adding the cask's flavor characteristics—including vanilla, caramel, tropical fruit, and charred wood—to its own.

When aged for two to eleven months, tequila earns the designation *reposado*, this being the category of most interest to slow sippers and makers of stirred cocktails. After a year in the barrel a tequila becomes an *añejo* (meaning aged), and at this point the bourbon-like caramels are well developed, while the distinctive tequila funk will be receding. A relatively new designation called *extra añejo* has been created to recognize tequilas that have sat in wood for more than two years; these should prove to be quite mellow indeed.

What brands to try? There are many fine tequilas, and I find it difficult to be too particular as long as the 100 percent agave rule is religiously observed. But if you must have recommendations, among the popular brands I regularly stock Tromba, Don Julio, and Herradura as everyday sipping tequilas, while El Jimador makes a capable and affordable go-to for the cocktail bar.

When you're meditatively sipping tequila, put aside the salt and lime. Do as the Mexicans and alternate between sips of tequila and nips of sangrita. Note the *t*; this is a concentrated, spicy citrus concoction quite different from the better-known Spanish sangria. Stir together equal parts freshly squeezed orange and lime juice, half as much grenadine, and Chohula hot sauce to taste. Chill for an hour and serve next to tequila, in tiny glasses.

ESSENTIAL TEQUILA COCKTAILS

Paloma

Paloma means "dove" in Spanish, and the name is a hint about its primary virtue: The simple mixture of tequila and grapefruit soda with a squeeze of lime turns turbulent tequila into something soft and easy to approach. Just start with 1½ ounces of 100 percent agave tequila in a highball glass with ice and fill with grapefruit soda and a squeeze of lime. It's so simple I'm not sure it even qualifies as a cocktail. Anyway, this is something Mexicans actually drink, as opposed to margaritas—which, while delicious, are actually an American invention and mark you as a gringo.

Margarita

The margarita seems to have originated on the U.S. side of the border, and it's possible there was no person named Margarita in the picture: The recipe resembles a much older American cocktail no one drinks anymore that was called the daisy, and *margarita* happens to be the Spanish word for "daisy."

Whether served at boring chain pubs, neighborhood Tex-Mex joints, or schlocky theme bars in Las Vegas, most of the margaritas that now come into this world exhibit serious defects, two of them maddeningly recurrent: too much sugar, and too much ice.

Ice melts quickly in the heat, which dilutes the drink and softens the crucial sting of the margarita. Instead of loading the drink up with ice, go back to its original form, straight up—meaning shake, strain, and leave no ice behind in the glass. And, yes, as with a daiquiri, I'm suggesting you at least try leaving the blender out of the picture. Use fresh juice (as always), never instant margarita mix, and serve it in a chilled stemmed glass, ideally a small version of the famous margarita variety, which bartenders also call coupettes.

Don't use ordinary table salt for the rim. Kosher salt is preferable. Better yet, if you've ever been tempted by the expensive, flaky sea salts (Maldon Salt and so on) at the grocery store, a margarita party is your excuse to spring for them.

Finally, for the orange flavor you can employ Cointreau or Grand Marnier. The former tastes cleaner and lighter while the latter yields a rounder, sweeter drink.

Margarita

- Freshly squeezed lime juice, for rimming the glass
- Flaky salt, for rimming the glass
- 1 ounce 100 percent agave tequila
- 1 ounce Cointreau or Grand Marnier
- 1 ounce freshly squeezed lime juice
- Lime wedge, for garnish (optional)

Dip the rim of a chilled cocktail glass in lime juice and then into a plate of salt to coat it. If you're serving a round to guests, salt just half the rim, to give them the opportunity to sip from a salt-free side if desired. Add the tequila, Cointreau, and lime juice to a cocktail shaker with ice and shake well. Strain into the prepared glass. Garnish with a lime wedge if you'd like.

Mezcal

Think of mezcal as tequila's authentic country cousin. They're both made by fermenting agave (albeit a different species, *Agave americana* in this case, known in Spanish as *maguey*). Unlike the tequila industry, which is big business, mezcal is still generally a back-woods affair involving haphazard-looking implements and practices: clay and bamboo stills rather than copper in some cases, plastic buckets, and a big one of these ‾_(ツ)_/‾ to the potentially expensive problem of stray microorganisms landing in the fermenting brew. You might spot burros pulling stone wheels to crush the charbroiled maguey. There's even a subvariety of mezcal called pechuga, which involves sticking a raw chicken carcass in the brew (if you're alarmed, bear in mind that alcohol is a disinfectant).

The result can taste, to haters at least, like a mixture of tequila, gasoline, and bear spray. Mezcal is not for the lily of liver. It's deep, moody stuff—something to drink during a summer rainstorm.

Not that I need to dissuade you from jumping right in, but when served mezcal, take tiny sips, never big gulps. Evidently, toasting one another somewhat elaborately is the way things are done in mezcal's home region of Oaxaca. No doubt the tradition grew up around the need to take it slow.

How to Drink Absinthe

I drank absinthe once. I tried to steal a police car.

—A GUY I KNEW IN NEWFOUNDLAND

W E ARE MEANT TO HEAR a summons to madness when, in the 2010 film *Get Him to the Greek*, Russell Brand's character, a louche, latter-day Keith Richards act-alike, asks Jonah Hill's rotund worrier: "Have you ever drunk absinthe? Like, from the 1900s?"

Absinthe enjoys a reputation as the tipple of scofflaws, the mythic libation of the Bohemian likes of Vincent van Gogh and Henri de Toulouse-Lautrec, with a badass danger factor located somewhere between shoplifting and snorting cocaine.

I hate to burst your bubble (just kidding: I actually love it), but that's all just mythology.

As a drinks writer I get asked about absinthe quite often, so I have the facts—which tell a tale quite different from the urban mythology—well rehearsed. Deep breath. Here goes: The undeservedly notorious herbal spirit known as absinthe is legal in the United States, Canada, Britain, and indeed most countries. It was banned in the States in 1912, but New Orleans–based distiller and chemist Ted Breaux persuaded the feds that the wormwood levels in a traditional recipe are far lower than people had always just assumed. In 2007, the authorities swallowed Breaux's arguments and relegalized the stuff. A flood of absinthe followed, and while the vogue has subsided, absinthe has settled into place as an everyday bar ingredient.

Absinthe is really just another licorice-flavored after-dinner spirit from the Mediterranean. These are legion, from the ouzos of Greece to the anises of Spain to the araks and rakis of Israel, Turkey, and Lebanon. Anisette, tsipouro, mastika, sambuca: All are flavored with aniseed, licorice, or both. Absinthe is traditionally French and Swiss; and in France, it coexists with lighter, sweeter (but equally licoricey) pastis.

Contrary to what some people insist on believing no matter what I tell them, today's absinthe contains just as much wormwood as the old stuff did. Yes, the genuine *Artemisia absinthium*. For some puzzling reason people always expect me to say that the absinthe you buy now is not the "real" absinthe. But unless it comes from eastern Europe, it probably is.

However—and once again this will disappoint some of you— the wormwood is in there to impart bitterness and balance against the dominant anise flavor, not to spark a hallucinatory thrill ride. Whatever you may read online, wormwood is not a hallucinogen, at least not in the quantities present in absinthe.

However, absinthe does contain plenty of an ingredient that will have crazy effects on your body and mind. It's called alcohol. Most absinthes reside in the 55% to 70% ABV range (other spirits tend to sit at the 40% mark). Go easy: You're not fooling around at that point. I suppose we can forgive those old French guys for thinking they were tripping.

> ABSINTHE DOES CONTAIN PLENTY OF AN INGREDIENT THAT WILL HAVE CRAZY EFFECTS ON YOUR BODY AND MIND. IT'S CALLED ALCOHOL.

The traditional method for serving absinthe involves slowly dripping cold water into it until it reaches your desired level of dilution. You might be able to see that magic moment arrive. Right before your eyes, the spirit will turn milky and cloudy—or "louche" in the parlance of absinthe enthusiasts. When anise-containing spirits turn cloudy it's called the ouzo effect, and it's the result of the hydrophobic compound known as anethole grouping into larger and larger clusters as water is added.

This alters the way light passes through the liquid.

While adding water, some will place a sugar cube in the midst of the stream to add sweetness to the liquor at the same time. I find that a quality absinthe requires no such adulteration. Anyway, absinthe spoons exist for the purpose of holding the sugar cube in place.

There's also a flaming sugar cube "ritual" going around; I understand it has no historical basis, being an invention out of whole cloth by eastern European absinthe marketers in the 1990s. Or so goes the narrative of the absinthe geeks (a robust tribe, easy to find if you Google around), who abhor the practice. I see no harm in it, but the cold water thing yields tastier results.

Now, which absinthe to try? I've gotten into trouble in the past for suggesting that the absinthes of eastern Europe—in the so-called Bohemian style—are anything less than the real deal, but they're certainly not where you go looking for a quality experience. Some sound advice for the absinthe newbie, at the risk of stepping into it again: You probably want to try one from North America, France, or Switzerland first. And maybe just stay there forever. I personally love Nouvelle-Orléans (France), La Clandestine (Switzerland), and Vieux Pontarlier (France again). Kübler and Pernod are more common, meanwhile, and just fine.

Death in the Afternoon

Ernest Hemingway is credited (blamed?) for inventing this drink, which is just absinthe and champagne, and about as wise as inviting a sack of flour to the temple. Toward the end of a raucous cocktail party at my place one time, I shouted out that anyone who actually wanted a death in the afternoon as a nightcap was (a) totally bonkers and (b) merely had to raise a hand and I'd make one for them. Every hand went up. Sometimes people jump off a cliff just to feel the fall. To partake, pour a generous ½ ounce absinthe in the bottom of a champagne flute and top with well-chilled bubbly. Stand back and prepare to Snapchat the mayhem.

PART IV

■ ■ ■

DRINKS BY OCCASION

WHAT TO DRINK ON VARIOUS OCCASIONS, FROM SUNDAY BRUNCH TO NEW YEAR'S EVE

Why do I drink champagne for breakfast? Doesn't everyone?

—NOËL COWARD

OFTEN THE DIFFERENCE between an ordinary time and a really swell time is just the drinks. Here are some tips on what to serve when, all recommended based on past track record.

VALENTINE'S DAY AND OTHER ROMANTIC DINNERS

What to drink when romance is in the air? Red Burgundy or Barolo. And champagne, naturally.

ST. PATRICK'S DAY

St. Patrick's Day is my least favorite time to head to a bar because I'm a curmudgeon who despises a crowd. All those amateurs who go to a pub only a couple of times a year just get in your way. Do yourself a favor and stay home, ideally with some Irish stout that

isn't necessarily Guinness, and some Irish whiskey to enjoy before turning in early for the night. Or have a few friends over for brunch and make Irish coffee (this can be as simple as coffee + whiskey + canned whipped cream; fancier versions exist, and the secret to a good hot drink is always to add obscene heaps of sugar).

OLD MAN COCKTAILS FOR THE DIVE BAR

The most obvious approach at a place where the utmost care may not be taken over the freshness of the ingredients is to stick to shots and bottled beer. Draft is often a dicey proposition in bars that don't take pride in their beer service. If you don't clean the lines regularly, they get gummed up with all sorts of junk, and while I have been assured that it's an urban myth that dirty draft makes you sick, it still doesn't taste great. Even nice-looking pubs will have dirty draft if they can't be bothered to do things right.

If you're feeling especially adventuresome, you could dodge the dodgy draft by ordering the sort of cocktail that hard-boiled old men drank in the twentieth century. The cocktails that follow are rather old-school formulations that can be assembled from the sticky, dust-covered bottles that line the back bar. They're semi-forgotten in our century, but don't really deserve to be. Thank goodness hard liquor never goes bad, like people do. Do try to remember the ratios of the ingredients, because the bartenders certainly won't know them by heart.

B&B

A B&B is a beverage of Zen simplicity and perfection: Equal parts Bénédictine and the brandy of your choice, ideally cognac, with ice in a rocks glass. It's cold and warming at the same time, seems to suit every season except perhaps high summer, and hits you like a brick—which might be precisely what you want on some occasions. There is a premixed, bottled B&B product that might actually outsell Bénédictine itself, but I prefer to mix my own B&Bs.

Gimlet

No one knows where the name comes from, but it's a near certainty that the gimlet originated as a makeshift cure for what ailed the officers of the Victorian-era British Royal Navy, namely, the twin maritime threats of scurvy and boredom. While the men belowdecks kept a workaday buzz on thanks to their daily ration of rum, the officers maintained class distinction by sipping on gin. They paired it with lime cordial, the available source of scurvy-fighting vitamin C, and the rest is history. (Much of that history consists of appearances in Raymond Chandler novels.)

If you've ever wondered why the Rose's Lime Cordial label and the atomic chartreuse fluid within are both so recognizable, even if you've never tried the stuff, it's because it's been there at the edge of your vision and consciousness your whole life. At least in English-speaking countries, convenience and grocery stores keep it around for the few remaining gimlet fans who walk among us. To make a gimlet, combine gin and Rose's Lime Cordial in a mixing glass, stir with ice, and decant into a chilled cocktail glass. The traditional ratio was 1:1, but for the more sugar-averse palates of our century I will suggest a 2:1 or even 3:1 ratio of gin to Rose's. A lime wedge won't hurt. Some people make gimlets with vodka instead of gin, but that's some grim drinking there.

Rusty Nail

I don't care if you're some kind of NASA Poindexter and look the part, people will respect you just a little more if they see you order a rusty nail. Like all the best dive-bar drinks, it's a simple two-step of hard liquor and something else that can survive unrefrigerated for years, in this case Scotch and Drambuie (which is really just sweetened and flavored Scotch).

Some suggest a 1:1 ratio of Scotch to Drambuie. But unless you're an irredeemable sugar addict, I suggest starting with 4 parts Scotch (2 ounces) to 1 part Drambuie (½ ounce). For the Scotch, a good, affordable blend is perfect: say Ballantine's, Grant's, or The Famous Grouse. Stir with ice until cold and well diluted, and serve in a rocks glass with a twist of lemon peel.

Stinger

The stinger's origins are actually quite posh—evidently the Vanderbilts were known to favor stingers back in the day (they reportedly added absinthe to theirs, not usually part of the recipe). Yet I'm suggesting the stinger as a dive-bar drink because it's composed entirely of hard liquor and nearly impossible to mess up. It's also a fine winter cocktail generally.

Assuming you're not a Vanderbilt, a stinger is just cognac and white crème de menthe, served ice cold. It's as smooth as it sounds—a drink that glides down your gullet like a hyper kid on a toboggan. And indeed the stinger has been prescribed as a drink to consume in the event of emergency, when great haste is required.

In Tennessee Williams's 1966 novella *The Knightly Quest*, poor Violet "tossed down hers as fast as if she were putting out a fire in her stomach, and then she said to Gewinner, Why, Prince, you didn't drink enough of that stinger to keep a bird alive! Oh well, I'll finish it for you. So she tossed down Gewinner's stinger too."

Stinger

The one way you can mess up a stinger is to use too much crème de menthe. A little goes a long way. The Savoy Cocktail Book suggested a 3:1 ratio back in 1931, and I think that's about right.

- 2¼ ounces good brandy (ideally cognac)
- ¾ ounce crème de menthe

Chill a cocktail glass. Add the cognac and crème de menthe to a shaker filled halfway with cracked (broken) ice, shake hard, and strain into the prepared glass.

BRUNCH (ESPECIALLY MOTHER'S DAY)

While a bloody Mary is traditional at brunch (or bloody Caesar, if you're Canadian—it's similar but with added clam juice, and I'm not joking), I prefer a mimosa. The British term is buck's fizz. The name of this bubbly-and-orange-juice pick-me-up may change on either side of the pond, but whatever you call it, you'll want to be generous with the sparkling wine. Use crémant (no point in champagne, really), with a 2:1 ratio of juice to bubbly. It doesn't matter what order you put them in the glass (which should be a champagne flute, by the way), because you're going to gently stir them together anyway. Use only orange juice that you or your monkey butler personally squeezed, never from a carton if you can avoid it, and use a sieve or tea strainer to eighty-six the pulp. Even for pulp lovers, it's preferable for the orange juice in a mimosa to be unencumbered by solid matter to the greatest degree possible. Squeeze the juice well ahead of serving and get it cold in the fridge. A lukewarm mimosa is a tepid experience.

LAZY SUMMER DAYS

Ah, British summers. So volatile, and so unpleasant at the extremes. There's no air conditioning anywhere and people don't even know how to grill: The average English person standing at a barbecue looks as confused as a monkey at a cash machine. Whatever the food is I can guarantee it'll be overcooked just to be on the safe side, because the British have yet to be persuaded that meat cooked outdoors will not strike them instantly dead.

Yet there's one thing that proves the British aren't completely useless at summer: Pimm's No. 1 Cup. It's so bloody delicious, it redeems them entirely. And knowing your way around Pimm's is one of the essential tools of the complete drinker.

Pimm's No. 1 Cup is a gin-based liqueur. No one drinks it on its own, although to do so is not unpleasant: You encounter a light-bodied liqueur with flavors of orange peel and sweet tea layered over the gin base. James Pimm invented his namesake liqueur at his London oyster bar in the mid-nineteenth century. His No. 1 Cup spread through time and space from there, but remains the most English of drinks, a point its advertising pluckily pounds home.

So Pimm's no. 1 cup is the name of the drink most commonly prepared from the liqueur named Pimm's No. 1 Cup. Try not to be confused.

A prepared glass of Pimm's generally consists of the namesake liqueur, an optional additional little hit of gin (something for those slightly naughty brunches), and a mixer, usually "lemonade" in the British sense (*lemonade* is British for lemon-lime sodas such as Sprite and 7 Up, and does not denote flat lemonade in the North American sense). The garnishes represent three-quarters of the joy of a Pimm's. Your glass ought to be festooned with some combination of lemon, orange, strawberry, mint, and cucumber. Remember the cucumber especially.

A Pimm's cup goes down incredibly easily, knocks thirst flat, and shows splendidly on social media. Pair with strawberries, watermelon, raw oysters, sunshine, and/or pure summery happiness.

After much (perhaps a little too much) experimentation, here's my procedure for a smashing good Pimm's. The "lemonade" I personally recommend is the fancy French kind that you'll find at gourmet food shops, which often comes in swing-top bottles. If you're entertaining, it's even smarter to scale this all up—say, quintuple everything—and make a big jug of Pimm's all at once.

Basic Pimm's Cup

- Mint sprigs
- 5–6 very thin slices of English cucumber
- Sparkling French lemonade
- 1½ ounces Pimm's
- 1 strawberry
- 1 long piece of English cucumber peel
- Small chunks of lemon and orange (optional)

1. Take a sprig or two of mint and put them at the bottom of a Collins glass. Put five or six very thin slices of English cucumber in there with it.

2. Add a splash of the French lemonade and gently press the cucumber and mint with a muddler or spoon to draw the flavors out. Now add the Pimm's and stir with a barspoon, stir stick, or chopstick.

3. Fill the glass with ice cubes. Top up with additional lemonade. Stir again, gently.

4. Garnish, if you please, with a fresh-looking sprig of mint, a strawberry, and/or a long piece of cucumber peel (use your vegetable peeler to make this). Drink straight from the glass: A straw only discourages you from breathing in the full aroma. Many people add chunks of citrus fruit as well, and this is fine but not necessary.

In a hurry? Fancy an option for a quickie Pimm's? The same gourmet grocers who stock your French sparkling lemonade are likely these days to carry cucumber soda as well. (It's tastier than it sounds.) Add some of that to your Pimm's in a tall glass with ice and whatever citrus chunks you can scare up and you've got yourself a fast makeshift patio refreshment.

SUMMER PARTIES

A tray of mint juleps nicely elevates a hot-weather shindig; make them ahead of time and keep them in the fridge until guests start to arrive. For a larger and more unruly group, try a make-your-own caipirinha station (see page 186). Or how about some more cups?

Mint Julep

For each julep, put 1 heaping teaspoon of granulated or quick-dissolving sugar, a splash of water, and a sprig of fresh mint in the bottom of a large glass. Press the mint gently into the sugar using a muddler or spoon. Stir to dissolve the sugar. Some undissolved granules may remain; that's fine. Add about 3 ounces of bourbon, cognac, or good Jamaican rum (try Appleton Estate). Yes, per drink. Some say 4 ounces. Giddy up.

Ginger Ale Cup

- 1 lemon, sliced
- Juice of 1 orange
- 4 ounces French brandy (need not be expensive)
- 2 ounces Luxardo maraschino liqueur or Bénédictine
- 1½ liters chilled ginger ale

Add the lemon slices, orange juice, brandy, maraschino, and ginger ale to a large pitcher with large ice cubes and stir gently until cold. Note the advice of the late Frank Meier: "A few sprigs of fresh mint may advisedly be added to most cups."

Peach Cup

- 1 ripe peach, carefully peeled and chopped
- 1 tablespoon powdered sugar (aka icing or confectioner's sugar)
- 1 bottle chilled Riesling
- ½ bottle decent but cheap dry sparkling wine (such as a French crémant), chilled

Add the peach chunks to the bottom of a large pitcher and pour in the sugar and half the Riesling. Put the pitcher in the fridge and wait 30 minutes for the flavors to mingle. Add the rest of the Riesling and the sparkling wine just before serving. An extra dash of powdered sugar added just before serving will make the cup froth dramatically.

CHRISTMAS

Traditional beverages for winter holidays include port and Madeira, sweet sherry, and good cognac.

Eggnog

Eggnog may be the most fun choice among your options. This recipe makes around 10 ounces—enough for one massive serving or two reasonable ones; use whatever glasses you feel like. The spirit can be up to you as well: Bourbon, dark rum, and cheap French brandy all work well. A fifty-fifty mix of Bénédictine and rum as the spirit component is sublime.

- 2 ounces (maximum) of your booze of choice
- 2 whole eggs
- 1 tablespoon powdered sugar (aka icing or confectioner's sugar)
- 4 ounces light cream (18% milk fat; in Canada, that's table cream; in the UK, single cream)
- Pinch of freshly grated nutmeg

Combine the booze, eggs, powdered sugar, and cream in a cocktail shaker without ice and shake vigorously until your arms tire and the egg has broken down into a smooth froth. This will take at least one minute, but go longer if you can. Add ice and shake some more, until the mixture is cold. Strain into one or two glasses. Before serving, toss a pinch of nutmeg across the top, if desired.

WINTER GET-TOGETHERS GENERALLY

I come from a country that, if you'll pardon our local expression, gets cold enough to break the balls off a brass monkey. You'd think we'd be experts at winter drinking, but we're not. I would like my fellow Canadians to pay special attention here (that goes for all you other cold-climate North Americans—I'm looking at you, Minnesota and North Dakota). Never drink a freezing cold lager on a freezing cold day again.

MULLED WINE

Mulled wine involves taking one of humanity's favorite grape-based beverages, heating it up to toasty, and adding lovely winter spices, rekindling warm memories of past holiday treats. What's not to love? Oh, right. The flavor.

I don't know about you, but I don't love mulled wine. But while most of the versions you'll come across at parties will tend to be vile, I find the following recipe—which I slaved over in my very own kitchen and is a synthesis of other renditions—tasty enough. By the way, if you don't have cheesecloth you can use a tea strainer ball for the herbs instead if you have one big enough.

Create a makeshift bag of spices by tying up in a piece of cheesecloth the peel of ½ orange, 1 cinnamon stick, and any combination of the following spices: ½ teaspoon chopped fresh ginger-root, ½ teaspoon freshly grated nutmeg, 5 crushed cloves, and 5 crushed cardamom pods. Add to a nonreactive pan (for example, an enameled one) with a full bottle of light red wine (Gamay Noir, for example) and ½ cup brown sugar. Yes, that's a lot of sugar: As always, copious sweetening is the secret to a successful hot drink. Heat slowly and stir. When it's steaming but not yet boiling, add 2 ounces of brandy, stir again, and serve with lemon wedges.

Hot Buttered Rum

You can find a lot of recipes for hot toddies out there if you search; they're typically a brown spirit plus sugar, cinnamon, maybe cloves, and lemon juice. While it's a little more complicated, I prefer hot buttered rum. This is a recipe I've adapted from Toronto's Martini Club.

- Orange slices
- Whole cloves
- 1½ ounces dark Jamaican rum
- ¼ ounce amaretto
- ¼ ounce Grand Marnier
- 1 ounce freshly squeezed lemon juice
- 1 teaspoon cherry brandy (optional)
- Hot black tea
- ¼ teaspoon unsalted butter

Stud the orange slices with the cloves by jamming the sharp side of the spice into the fruit rind. To a large heatproof mug, add the rum, amaretto, Grand Marnier, lemon juice, cherry brandy, and 1 whole clove. Top with the hot black tea and stir. Add the butter. Drop the studded orange slices into the drink.

Glögg

Have you ever noticed the glögg stuff they sell in the food section at IKEA? It actually tastes pretty good if you add brandy and cloves to give it a bit of a kick. Or try mulled cider (gently warm nonalcoholic cider, add cinnamon and cloves to taste, stir in brown sugar to taste, chuck in bourbon at the end). Everybody loves that.

NEW YEAR'S EVE

If you're entertaining on New Year's Eve, I find a big bowl of the champagne cup pleases a crowd. My recipe is a modernization of an old number from London's storied Savoy Hotel. For the sparkling wine, use actual champagne if entertaining aristocrats. For commoners, cava or crémant will do just fine.

Champagne Cup

- 2 bottles well-chilled sparkling wine
- 6½ ounces Grand Marnier
- 1½ ounces maraschino liqueur (or substitute amaretto, if necessary)
- Peel of an English cucumber, in long pieces
- Peel of 1 lemon
- 1 orange, sliced
- ¼ pineapple, cut in chunks
- 4 teaspoons powdered sugar (aka icing or confectioner's sugar)
- Mint leaves that guests can add themselves (optional); serve in a separate bowl

Add the wine, Grand Marnier, maraschino, cucumber peel, lemon peel, orange slices, and pineapple chunks to a large serving container with large ice cubes and stir well. Add the powdered sugar, which will reinvigorate the bubbles somewhat. Serve with the mint leaves on the side.

French 75

Another sparkling option, suitable for a smaller group, is to serve a round of French 75s. Named after a World War I machine gun, and as deadly as the allusion is meant to suggest. Makes a terrific way to stretch a bottle of bubbly that doesn't have enough juice left for everyone to get a real glass.

- 2 ounces gin
- 1 ounce freshly squeezed lemon juice
- 1 teaspoon powdered sugar (aka icing or confectioner's sugar)
- Champagne or other dry sparkling wine, to top
- Twist of lemon peel (optional)

Add the gin, lemon juice, and sugar to a cocktail shaker with ice. Shake well. Strain the mixture into a champagne flute, top with champagne. Garnish with a lemon twist, if desired.

APERITIFS, TO DRINK
BEFORE DINNER

It has the power, rare with drinks and indeed with anything else, of cheering you up.

—KINGSLEY AMIS, ON THE NEGRONI COCKTAIL

MONG THE MANY MYSTERIOUS REGIONS of the local liquor store, few are as perplexing to the spirits novice as the row (or corner) where a certain class of continental concoctions awaits you. If you're sufficiently distant from the multicultural cram of a big city or a cluster of southern European immigrants, you might need to wipe a layer of dust off

the bottles to reveal the pure red of Campari, the faded Renaissance shades of green and yellow in the bottles of Chartreuse, or the cartoonishly bright orange of Aperol. The brand names are boldly and proudly stated—these bottles swagger out as if they're a big deal somewhere, and believe them, they really are. They're bigger in France or Italy (or wherever) than you can likely imagine.

Congratulations, you've stumbled into the arcane world of European herbal and bitter liqueurs, whose primary purpose in this world is to make Europeans feel as if what they are drinking isn't merely booze but part of a wholesome culinary regime. Most of the products we're talking about here play a role in daily European life as aperitifs (aperitivos) and digestifs (digestivos). These French (Italian) names betray their origins in the Mediterranean and their roots in deeply held, but scientifically questionable, southern European beliefs about the medicinal properties of certain alcoholic drinks.

Most of the famous aperitifs and digestifs originated in the golden age of quackery, remnants of a time when snake oils promising digestive relief were sold without legal restriction. People formulated and drank them as a weapon in the timeless war against tummy trouble.

Here's how it works: A proper southern European meal begins with an aperitif. That's the French term and the one we usually employ in English; *aperitivo* is Italian. Either way, the word comes from the Latin *aperire*, which means "to open." The alcoholic load of the product tends to be moderate—say, 10% to 30%, and at the higher end you tend to dilute it when serving. It could be a glass of dry wine, such as sherry or champagne, or it will be a product that's specially designed for premeal imbibing. In this case, it will often contain the aforementioned botanical brew of herbs, roots, spices, and flowers. People swear these work as a preventative measure against stomach distress, and yet most of the ingredients are secret and the formulas tightly restricted.

Of course that tempts the booze geeks to go guessing and investigating the recipe. One tries to sniff out a whiff of gentian here or thyme there. But confirming these suspicions? Short of staging a *Mission: Impossible* break-in and stealing the ancient manuscripts that reveal the liqueur's recipe—or the invoices for the ingredients, which is what I'd try—we'll never know what's in the bottle. So there's no point guessing at it, and you're better off sitting back and enjoying each sip as a harmonious experience in itself.

Bookending a meal by starting and finishing it with specialized booze has become trendy enough outside southern Europe that it's no rarity to see Italian digestifs in the United Kingdom and North America, even in restaurants and bars that have nothing to do with Mediterranean cuisine (there's even a bar in Chicago called Billy Sunday that has a digestif list and a deep cellar of the stuff, presented the way a fine restaurant does with wine). The discovery of aperitifs by English speakers was probably driven by the intriguing bittersweet flavors and romance of sunny southern Europe, not beliefs about the workings of the digestive system. However, I admit to reaching for Fernet-Branca when my guts rumble. It can't hurt, can it?

Maybe the Mediterranean obsession with digestion is just an excuse to drink. From a certain point of view, an herbal liqueur is the spiritual ancestor of the gluten-free cookie: Supposedly beneficial for one's health, but often enjoyable even if all the claims turn out to be rubbish anyway. In this chapter, I introduce some of the most popular European aperitifs and suggest a few widely practiced ways to prepare and enjoy them. There are always multiple serving options, but these will work as a starting point.

Among aperitifs that have their own chapters elsewhere in this book, vermouth makes a splendid meal starter when fresh and served on the rocks with a twist of orange, if sweet, or lemon, if dry. (For more on this wine, see page 66.) Dry sherry works especially well with salty foods, seafood, and/or anything Spanish in origin. Look for the words *fino, manzanilla,* or *amontillado* on the label to find a sherry that will suit. And any quality sparkling wine (including cava and prosecco) works well as an aperitif, too. Bon appétit.

CAMPARI

How to drink: Mix about 1½ ounces Campari with at least twice as much soda; serve with a twist or slice of orange or make a negroni (see below).

While the color of Campari—as red as red gets—is universally appealing, this Italian liqueur is one of those culinary experiences that divides the human population into two bitterly opposed halves. To some, the slightly citric tartness of Campari is simply unbearable. For others, it's not only irresistible, it's an indispensible ritual. And even those who adore Campari will soften the blow with soda or the velvety cloak of a negroni. Although it tastes as bitter as an amaro, you always drink Campari before dinner, never after. Rivals/alternatives include Luxardo Bitter and Gran Classico.

NEGRONI

I'd be willing to wager that most of the Campari consumed outside Italy goes into negronis, a cocktail invented by an eccentric Florentine aristocrat in the early twentieth century (among other activities, he traveled around the States as a rodeo curiosity). They're quite popular in the English-speaking world.

Countless formulas circulate, but, like many other lovers of Italian aperitifs, I prefer the Euclidian elegance of a 1:1:1 ratio between gin, Campari, and (fresh) sweet vermouth. I like to take a rocks glass and put about three medium-size ice cubes in it, add all the liquids, and stir until cold. Then I add a twist or slice of orange—or, if I'm feeling like a flourish, both. Not into the whole precision thing? That's all right, too. There's a school of thought that says you can't really mess up a negroni. As cocktail guru Gaz Regan, who wrote a whole book about negronis, promised: "You can slap my wrist and call me Deborah if it doesn't also work with whatever ratios you use."

APEROL

How to drink: Mix 1½ to 2 ounces Aperol with at least twice as much soda; serve with a twist or slice of orange or make an Aperol spritz (see page 228).

Italy's best-selling spirit, Aperol bears a family resemblance to Campari. They're both made by the same company, Gruppo Campari, but Aperol is a great deal lighter—11% alcohol, while Campari is around 24% (the precise strength varies by export country). Aperol offsets the bite of quinine with plenty of sweet citrus. If you find Campari too much to handle, even with soda, Aperol could work as a gateway drug.

You don't see people drinking Aperol on its own. It tends to go into a spritz with prosecco and soda. While the Aperol spritz is made from Italian ingredients, it's just as Austrian as it is Italian. (You see the telltale bright orange of an Aperol spritz on virtually every outdoor patio table in Vienna in the springtime.)

Aperol Spritz

Use the alternate amounts, listed in parentheses, to give your insides more of a spritzing than usual.

- 1½ (2) ounces Aperol
- 2 (3) ounces prosecco or other dry sparkling wine
- Splash of club soda, to taste
- 1 slice of orange, for garnish

Combine and gently stir the Aperol, prosecco, and club soda in a wine or rocks glass with ice and serve with a slice of orange

PASTIS

> *How to drink: Add 5 parts cool water to 1 part pastis (say, 1½ ounces) in a tall glass.*

As you can read in the chapter on absinthe, the notorious spirit was (needlessly) outlawed in France in 1915. This left an opening for a new anise-flavored liquor to sashay into the golden hour of the Provençal afternoon. Pastis is absinthe-esque in the clear, insistent brightness of its licorice flavor, but sweeter than absinthe, and it lacks wormwood. Ricard and Pernod eventually became the top brands (you'll also see Baranis and 51, especially in France). When you're drinking pastis, you generally don't drink it straight; you add about 5 measures of cool water per 1 measure of pastis. You'll notice the ouzo effect, which makes it turn opaque (see page 203).

Pastis belongs to a whole family of anise-flavored liquors from around the Mediterranean: There's ouzo from Greece, sambuca and anisette from Italy, arak from Lebanon, and so on. Some Turkish rakis are all right, but for grace and sophistication in the licorice liquor category, I don't think you can beat Ricard pastis.

LILLET

How to drink: Serve about 3 ounces on the rocks with twist of orange.
Lillet has spent its existence in the shadows of the other, flashier wines of Bordeaux. You probably can't fault the planet for mostly overlooking Lillet and focusing instead on some of the finest wines humanity has ever uncorked. But we should spare a thought or two for the self-described "aperitif de Bordeaux," a fortified wine you could think of as a sweeter, fruitier cousin of vermouth. Lillet Blanc is an ingredient in a number of cocktails, the two most common being the vesper and the twentieth century. And if you're feeling a bit dead, try a corpse reviver.

Corpse Reviver No. 2

Lillet forms the soft backbone to this refreshing cocktail, likely a creation of London's Savoy Hotel circa the 1920s and the lone popular survivor of a once-diverse category of "corpse reviver" cocktails. They're meant to be hangover cures, which may help to explain the joke behind the name.

- 1 ounce dry gin
- 1 ounce Lillet Blanc
- 1 ounce Cointreau
- 1 ounce freshly squeezed lemon juice
- 2–3 drops absinthe (or pastis)

Add all the ingredients to a cocktail shaker filled halfway with ice and shake well. Strain into a chilled cocktail glass.

Dubonnet

Serve about 3 ounces on the rocks with a twist of lemon, or with gin as directed below

Dubonnet Rouge is made with Grenache, Muscat, and Carignan grapes and aged in oak with natural flavors such as orange peel, coffee beans, quinine, and—of course—"secret spices." You could think of Dubonnet as broadly similar to sweet vermouth, but it's far sweeter, much less bitter, and vaguely chocolatey, with some wintry flavors. It's a favorite of the British royal family; there was a bit of a kerfuffle at Lord's Cricket Ground in 2009 when Queen Elizabeth was in attendance to take in the action; her majesty wanted Dubonnet to drink, but none of the liquor stores nearby had any.

Dubonnet may be sticky-sweet coming out of the bottle, but in-the-know Dubonnet fans (which can't just be me and some octogenarian Englishwomen, can it?) know that it's delightful when cut with ice, gin, and lemon peel. Dubonnet goes well with a wide variety of spirits, not just gin, and figures in a number of cocktails dreamed up between 1910 and 1940. Here's one:

Dubonnet Cocktail

- 1½ ounces Dubonnet
- 1½ ounces gin (try Plymouth, Bulldog, or Beefeater)
- Twist of lemon peel

Stir Dubonnet and gin in a mixing glass with ice and strain into a small, chilled cocktail glass. Squeeze a small piece of lemon peel over the drink and drop into the glass.

Some versions of this recipe include ¼ ounce freshly squeezed lemon juice. That's too sour for me, but go ahead and try it. I also like to add a dash or two of lavender bitters.

KIR AND KIR ROYALE

It wasn't Félix Kir who invented Dijon's gift to the apéro hour, but he certainly deserves the honor of having the drink named after him. It was at least a century ago that the locals adopted the practice of mixing two local products, crème de cassis (that is, blackcurrant liqueur) with Aligoté, a parchment-dry white wine. Kir was a priest and resistance fighter who survived the Nazis to become mayor of Dijon after the war. He made a point of pressing a cassis and wine into the hand of many a visiting dignitary, and that's how it came to be known as a "kir."

A kir is best when made with 1 part crème de cassis to 4 parts dry white wine, especially Aligoté. But you can use any dry white wine.

A kir royale is made with French sparkling wine rather than still, and in my view, 1 part crème de cassis to 6 parts champagne or crémant makes for a stellar one. Do try to use honest-to-goodness champagne, not mere crémant—this is one instance where I really think it's worth the extra cost. The biscuity dryness of champagne just plain works with jammy cassis. A kir royale made with prosecco, conversely, doesn't turn out well in my experience—too sweet.

DIGESTIFS,
FOR AFTER DINNER

"Perhaps we should have a drink." [Rinaldi] opened his
trunk and took out a bottle.
"Not Strega," I said.
"No. Grappa."
"All right."

—ERNEST HEMINGWAY, *A FAREWELL TO ARMS*

THE END-OF-MEAL COUNTERPART of the aperitif is the digestif, meant to "warm" the stomach to aid digestion *after* a meal. This may be a holdover of the ancient belief, which dates back to the Romans, that the stomach "cooks" your food a second time as you digest.

Among spirits that were specially designed as digestifs, France gives us Chartreuse and a host of more obscure options, most of them quite difficult to track down outside that country. It's the Italians who have really conquered the world market in digestifs. Foreigners have learned to enjoy submitting to the self-flagellatory pleasures of shutting down the digestion factory with a cloyingly-sugared-yet-tongue-dryingly-bitter glass of amaro. That's a category of brown liquors that taste like medicine even to ardent admirers.

Other hard liquors with which you're already familiar are also served as digestifs, which explains their location at the back of restaurant menus: Commonly used in this way are grappa, cognac, whiskey, armagnac, and calvados. Scotch is surprisingly popular in the Mediterranean. France is the world's greatest consumer of

Scotch whisky per capita, and the digestif ritual probably explains why.

Finally, digestifs should come after any sweet dessert wines (Sauternes, vin santo, Pedro Ximénez sherry, for example), not before.

As with aperitifs, I've highlighted a few well-known digestif options and noted one or two easy ways to serve them.

AMARO

How to drink: 1 or 2 two ounces amaro neat or with a splash of cool water. Also found in cocktails.

A little glass of amaro is an authentically Italian way to end a meal. Amari (that's the plural) are concoctions of alcohol, sugar, and botanicals. They're made right up and down Italy's boot and each brand has its own characteristic flavor, from the burnt sugar emphasis of Averna to the fresh herbal mountain blast of Braulio.

While there are premium brands out there (Sibilla and Nonino, for example), most amaro is delightfully cheap. It's a savvy tactic to order amaro at the end of a restaurant meal to try to keep the total down. "Who's up for amaro?" you call out. "Show of hands." No one will suspect you're just desperate to keep a bunch of Johnnie Walker Blues from showing up on the bill.

"Fernet" is usually treated as a sort of subcategory of amaro—the bitterest of a bitter bunch, with less sugar. By far the most popular brand is Fernet-Branca, but there are alternatives, including Letherbee fernet of Chicago, which is so bitter it may cause the vestigial forest primate part of your brain to shriek in panic at the threat of poisoning as you force down each tiny, potently puckering sip. Fernet appears in cocktails, too, the best known of which is named for my hometown.

Toronto Cocktail

- 2 ounces rye whisky, ideally Canadian
- ¼ ounce Fernet-Branca or other fernet
- ¼ ounce simple syrup
- 2 dashes Angostura bitters
- Twist of orange or lemon, for garnish

Combine the rye, fernet, simple syrup, and bitters with ice in a mixing glass. Stir and strain into a cocktail glass. Squeeze the citrus peel to spray the essential oils onto the surface of the drink and drop it into the glass.

JÄGERMEISTER AND ZWACK UNICUM

How to drink: Serve about 1½ ounces Jägermeister on the rocks or with cola.

It's not just the Italians who cap a gut-busting meal with inky-dark potions swirling with secret bitter herbs: Central Europe has essentially the same tradition. The most commercially successful brand by far is Germany's well-known Jägermeister, which is mostly familiar in North America (and I'm sure many other places) as a cheap rock 'n' roll bar shot. Jäger's popularity among rockers, the result of a brilliant marketing strategy by its 1970s American importer, can only be helped by packaging that looks undeniably badass. I don't suppose many people will sip Jäger in the digestif fashion no matter what I say, but I swear it's worth a try.

I'll mention Zwack Unicum, which is from Hungary, in passing, as a Jäger alternative that some will find a little more palatable and sophisticated.

Chartreuse

> *How to drink: serve 1 or 2 ounces Chartreuse neat or with a splash of cool water. Also a common cocktail ingredient.*

France's most famous herbal digestif is harmoniously mellow compared to some of its extremist Italian cousins. Made by Carthusian monks near Grenoble, it's a sweet and complex swirl of aloe, angelica, calamus, saffron, and a staggering 125 other undisclosed botanicals.

Chartreuse comes in two main varieties, which people call yellow and green (the labels for both just say "Chartreuse"). There are some expensive special editions as well. The regular old yellow, at 40% alcohol, is mellow and smells a little like marshmallow, which makes for a nice little rhyming mnemonic. Some of the floral and spicy aromas pop out at you when you add a little water.

The green seems to be more popular. I find green Chartreuse to be cleaner and fresher tasting than the yellow. It's like a gust of alpine air, while the yellow is like a dessert made out of sugar and flowers.

The Chartreuses both feature in a large number of cocktail recipes, often as little as a quarter ounce to add a gust of herbal flavor. The bijou is an example of a cocktail that does not hold back on the Chartreuse.

Bijou

- 1 ounce London dry gin
- 1 ounce sweet vermouth
- 1 ounce green Chartreuse
- 1–2 dashes orange bitters
- Twist of orange peel, for garnish

Stir the gin, vermouth, Chartreuse, and bitters with ice in a mixing glass and strain into a chilled cocktail glass. Garnish with the orange peel and serve.

STREGA

How to drink: Serve about 1½ ounces Strega on the rocks.

Strega is similar in color to yellow Chartreuse, and it makes an enjoyably bittersweet, floral, coniferously vegetal crescendo to a meal. It comes from Benevento, a town in the southern Italian region of Campania that teems with local witchcraft lore. The name means "witch," hence the witchy imagery on the packaging.

DRINKS THAT WORK EITHER BEFORE OR AFTER DINNER

Some products are switch-hitters, capable of serving as an aperitif or a digestif, depending on how they're served. Remember: This isn't an exact science, this aperitif/digestif thing—truth be told, it isn't science at all.

PUNT E MES

How to drink: Serve about 2 ounces of Punt E Mes on the rocks with a twist of orange. Also found in many cocktails, especially contemporary ones.

Punt E Mes usually falls into the vermouth category because it's wine based, but it is so syrupy and bitter, it can easily function as a digestif if taken neat and cool or with a small amount of ice.

CYNAR

How to drink: Serve about 2 ounces Cynar with a splash of cool water, or on the rocks with a twist of orange. Or with tonic and a twist of lemon.

Known for the big green artichoke on the label, Cynar is technically an amaro (and a relative latecomer; it debuted in 1952). People often think of it as a category unto itself, an "artichoke liqueur," because it contains cynarin, the essence of artichoke. To me, Cynar—which is pronounced chee-NAR—tastes nothing like artichoke. It's your garden-variety amaro: bitter with hints of burnt sugar. But playing up the artichoke angle exploits the ancient Italian belief that artichokes stimulate the functioning of the gallbladder and liver.

Cynar appears most often as a digestif, on the rocks. But you're encouraged to try it before dinner with soda and a twist, or as a spritz with prosecco and soda, or on the rocks with tonic water. I find the latter especially tasty.

BECHEROVKA

How to drink: Serve about 1½ ounces Becherovka with at least 3 ounces of tonic and a twist of lemon.

The Czech Republic's contribution to bitter liquors might have played its own part in the twentieth century's misfortunes: Britain's Lord Walter Runciman was Neville Chamberlain's envoy to Nazi Germany in the late 1930s, charged with discussions over the Sudetenland. Some have tried to blame his cocking up of those negotiations on his tendency to drink too much Becherovka. Perhaps he'd have swallowed anything. Try the stuff with ice, tonic, and a twist to see if you're similarly susceptible. Diluted and attenuated by the dry tang of quinine, Becherovka becomes an aromatic delight, one that dances with tonic every bit as nimbly as gin. Czechs call this mixture a *beton,* which means "concrete"—surely a hideous misnomer for such a sprightly palate cleanser.

AD-HOCTAILS, FOR
THOSE TIMES WHEN
YOU'RE TRULY DESPERATE

Improvising is wonderful. But, the thing is you can't
improvise unless you know exactly what you are doing.

—CHRISTOPHER WALKEN

IT'S AMONG THE WORST WAYS to find yourself at a
party: glumly fixing yourself round after round of the same
dreary highball—rum and cola, gin and tonic, whiskey and
ginger ale; whatever your favorite may be. You slide the ice
down the side of the plastic cup, eyeball the right amount of
spirit required to get through the next dull conversation, then
add enough mixer so that the spirit goes down without putting
up a fight. Drinking hardly ever descends to grimmer levels than
this. Yet we fall into it time and again because we were in a rush
getting ready for the shindig, or we are feeling less than creative,
or we had to stop in at a poorly provisioned place for supplies
along the way.

Friends, I have a happier alternative for those go-go nights
when nothing complicated is possible. I call it the ad-hoctail. It's a
traditional cocktail dumbed down to two or three easy-to-obtain
ingredients. It may be less delicious, but it's acceptable under the
circumstances.

Mojitos are complicated, right? All that measuring, squeezing,
stirring, and, of course, tracking down mint leaves. As a solution,
my brother invented something he calls the "ghetto mojito," which

is simply white rum plus lemon-lime soda (such as Sprite), proportions unimportant. If you're missing the flavor of mint, chew some gum. Result? Relaxing times, and you've put the best possible face on a rushed situation. Most important, you won't need to puzzle over the challenge of finding fresh mint on the way to the party.

Though it may lack in the areas of flavor balance and sophistication, the ad-hoctail more than makes up for its deficiencies by offering convenience, ingenuity, and sheer mixological moxie. It is simplicity embraced with gusto. It is the meeting place between thirst and a shrug.

CONVENIENCE, INGENUITY, AND SHEER MIXOLOGICAL MOXIE.

Take the Manhattan on $15 a day, one of my own rushed creations: It's nothing but North American whiskey—and, good lord, do not use the expensive stuff—and cherry cola, joined together and consumed with perverse pride. The dépanneur daiquiri (the name comes from the Canadian French for "convenience store") once helped me make friends at a party where I suddenly discovered that the people I had arrived with had departed. Discovering myself friendless, did I skulk out in embarrassment? No! Suddenly a stranger in a strange situation, I decided to make a strange drink. I fixed a round of easy fizzy daiquiris and made all new friends. Necessity is the mother of invention, and the dépanneur daiquiri was one mother of a solution.

THE RECIPES

Dépanneur Daiquiri

- White rum, ready-to-drink lemonade, sweet lime-flavored soda (like Lime Crush or Jarritos Lime). Use twice as much fake lime as fake lemon.

Manhattan on $15 a Day

- 1½ ounces Canadian whisky
- Cherry cola

Add ice and whisky to a rocks glass (if available) and swirl it around a bit. Fill the glass with cherry cola.

Un-Cosmopolitan

- 1½ ounces vodka
- Cherry Kool-Aid
- Orange soda

To a child's sippy cup, add ice, vodka, and Kool-Aid. Close the lid. Shake. Add a splash of orange soda and enjoy.

Off-White Russian No. 1

- 1 ounce vodka
- One 8-ounce (250-milliliter) carton of chocolate milk (that is, lunch-box size)

Pour the vodka into the chocolate milk carton. Close the spout. Shake. Drink through a straw, if available.

Off-White Russian No. 2

- • Vodka
- • Brand-name iced coffee

I would recommend the Mr. Brown brand of iced coffee for this; it's from Taiwan and comes in small cans. (Mr. Brown has put that little melamine scare behind him.) Another option, if you live in Canada or the northeastern United States: Tim Hortons makes iced coffee and of course the famous Iced Capp, so you can use those. Those Starbucks coffees in glass bottles will work but seem a bit too posh for our exercise here, so use only as a last resort. In terms of proportions, you're freestyling it here.

Sherribull (aka the Bull Sherrier)

Mix 1 part Red Bull with 1 part sherry. Among its virtues, the Sherribull will keep you awake. All right, that's the only virtue.

HOW TO MAKE AN OLD FASHIONED IN AN AIRPLANE (AND OTHER COCKTAILS YOU CAN MAKE ON THE FLY)

Cocktail supply stores now sell kits that you can carry onto a plane so that you can mix your own superior drinks in the air. If that's too much gear or foresight for you, locate and carry around tiny two-serving bottles of Angostura bitters for "emergencies." (I found some at thewhiskyexchange.com.) On your next plane trip, request whiskey on the rocks and a packet of sugar. I find that flight attendants are indulgent when it comes to the whims of people who smile and treat them with kindness, so be a mensch . . .

and then also request a little orange juice. Tip the juice (optional) into the cup with the whiskey, ice, and sugar, and stir. Pull the Angostura bitters out of your pocket for the finishing touch.

Another thing you could do with your tiny bottles of Angostura and sugar packets: Should you check into a hotel and discover an unfamiliar sparkling wine in your room's minibar or as a complimentary treat (this happens in Las Vegas)—and it turns out to be dreadful—elevate it into a makeshift champagne cocktail. Pour the sugar and Angostura into the bottom of the glass and fill with the offending bubbly. Not perfect, but perhaps it's an improvement.

Other ideas to keep in your back pocket: If you can scrounge up about ½ ounce of honey and two or three lemon wedges, add them to a glass, then gin (or, if you're in dire straits, vodka), and stir well. Now you have a bee's knees cocktail (sort of). Tell the people staring at you that it's a Prohibition-era cocktail, totally legit.

A batanga, meanwhile, is just tequila, lime juice, and cola (plus a salted rim in ideal circumstances). If you have tequila and can locate some lime wedges and a soda machine, you're sorted.

In general, by remembering your cocktail recipes, more or less, you can make out all right in all kinds of situations. One time at the KLM predeparture lounge at Toronto's Pearson Airport, I made an ad-hoc French 75 out of mediocre rosé sparkling wine, no-name brandy, a sugar packet from the coffee station, and lemon juice extracted from wedges found next to the bar area. You do what you have to do. If you can keep your head about you in everyday situations like this and improvise something half drinkable, and look almost suave while doing it, congratulations: You have become a complete drinker.

FURTHER READING

This book is meant as an introduction to better drinking. There is much more to know, and here are trustworthy sources that can teach it to you.

COCKTAILS

Berry, Jeff "Beachbum." *Potions of the Caribbean.* New York: Cocktail Kingdom, 2015. A specialized volume full of tiki drinks, from a true expert on the genre.

Clarke, Paul. *The Cocktail Chronicles.* Nashville: Spring House Press, 2015. Read this to get up to speed on what has happened in the world of cocktails during the present revolution, with recipes for playing along at home.

Craddock, Harry. *The Savoy Cocktail Book.* London: Pavilion Books, 1999 (reprint of 1930 edition). Of all the handy old cocktail books, this is the handiest.

Kaplan, David, Nick Fauchald, and Alex Day. *Death & Co.: Modern Classic Cocktails.* Berkeley: Ten Speed Press, 2014. Of all the aspirational new cocktail books, this one has the drinks to aspire to.

Morgenthaler Jeffrey, with Martha Holmberg. *The Bar Book.* San Francisco: Chronicle Books, 2014. Cocktail-making technique explored in fine detail, for those who really want to do it properly.

Wondrich, David. *Imbibe.* Rev. ed. New York: TarcherPerigee, 2015. The early history of cocktails as told through a detailed reexamination of the career and works of a showy nineteenth-century American barman, "Professor" Jerry Thomas, and how to make them well. The most useful book of all for getting your head around what cocktails are and where they come from.

Whiskey

Broom, Dave. *Whisky: The Manual.* London: Mitchell Beazley, 2014. A wonderful handbook for everyday whiskey drinking by a terrific fellow who is somewhat more into the whole idea of adding mixers than I am.

Buxton, Ian. *101 Whiskies to Try before You Die.* London: Hachette, 2010. The title says it all.

de Kergommeaux, Davin. *Canadian Whisky: The Portable Expert.* Toronto: McClelland & Stewart, 2012. Thorough and well written, a must for fans of Canadian whisky.

Other Spirits

Broom, Dave. *Gin: The Manual.* London: Mitchell Beazley, 2015. Good old Dave Broom again, up to his usual informative self.

Curtis, Wayne. *And a Bottle of Rum.* New York: Three Rivers Press, 2007. An absorbing history of rum, including the sobering chapters involving slavery.

Stewart, Amy. *The Drunken Botanist.* Chapel Hill: Algonquin Books, 2013. A fun romp through the plants that give their lives to make our liquor. Includes hints on what's in all those bitter European products.

Beer

Beaumont Stephen. *The Beer & Food Companion.* London: Jacqui Small, 2015. This is the only book about beer that the casual beer drinker needs: It gives you all the information you need to choose a few, and inspiration for what to drink it with, all delivered by the steady hand of a true expert.

WINE

Asimov, Eric, and Florence Fabricant. *Wine with Food: Pairing Notes and Recipes from the New York Times.* New York: Rizzoli, 2014. Practical advice on what to eat and what to wash it down with.

Baiocchi, Talia. *Sherry.* Berkeley: Ten Speed Press, 2014. An excellent book on an overlooked wine style.

Oldman, Mark. *Oldman's Guide to Outsmarting Wine.* London: Penguin Books, 2004. I use this thorough-yet-concise book as a day-to-day reference for what I'm drinking, or ought to drink.

Robinson, Jancis. *The Oxford Companion to Wine.* Oxford: Oxford University Press, 2015. Everything you ever wanted to know about wine and a gazillion other things you might want to look up one day, all in one inconveniently massive volume. Purchasing as an e-book may be wise, to save space.

Steinberger, Michael. *The Wine Savant.* New York/London: W.W. Norton & Company, 2013. An opinionated guide to current trends and thinking in wine; a valuable palate cleanser to help wash away some of the other, discouraging things you may have read.

DRINKING IN GENERAL

Amis, Kingsley. *Everyday Drinking.* New York: Bloomsbury USA, 2008. The book about drinks I've always wished I could write.

COCKTAIL SUPPLIERS

If you live in Canada, buy your drinks gear from byobto.com or thecraftybartender.com. If in the United States (or anywhere else in the world), also look at cocktailkingdom.com. If you're trying to track down those tiny Angostura bitters bottles, try thewhisky exchange.com.

ACKNOWLEDGMENTS

I'm grateful to my family and friends for serving as guinea pigs and occasional errand runners and suitcase booze smugglers on my behalf; I'll single out my mom for not grounding me too severely for my underage drinking escapades (which turned out to lead somewhere productive in the long run. It wasn't a wasted youth after all—right?).

Cheers to the people who put *The Social* on the air, especially Amber Buchanan, who found me, put me on the show, and produces most of my segments—and does so with such aplomb.

The features crew at the *National Post* deserves my gratitude for running my drinks columns since February 2006. Ben Errett gave me the chance to write the column, and it wouldn't have kept going for more than a decade if not for the support of Maryam Siddiqi, Barry Hertz, and Jessica Johnston.

I owe a debt of gratitude to my friend and former roommate (and dedicated pale lager drinker) Cherise Burda for putting up with the mountains of mysterious booze, non-dishwasher-able bar accoutrements, and sticky counters.

Thank you to all the people in the drinks world (distillers, brewers, and so on) who have helped me file more than five hundred booze columns. An especially big thanks to Canada's wonderful bartenders; there's another special salute to you on p. 173.

My editor at TarcherPerigee, Marian Lizzi, deserves a raised glass for agreeing that the world needed a new general primer for everyday drinking, and that I should be the person to write it. Then she turned out to be such a perceptive editor—and impressively quick! Lauren Appleton and Candace B. Levy also deserve my thanks for their hard work to bring this little project to fruition.

This book wouldn't look half as nifty in your hands had I not been able to secure the much-sought-after illustration services of Kagan McLeod. Not only is he the best at what he does (just look!), he's a pretty great MC too, as is well known to fans of Conrad Black Sabbath.

Thank you to the good people of The Rights Factory, especially my agent and friend, the very drink-savvy Kelvin Kong, for being such an ardent supporter of the concept and a pleasant bar companion.

The biggest toast of all goes to the wonderful Emily Game—maker of a pretty mean boulevardier and champagne cocktail herself—whose patience and taste-testing skills are above reproach. People often tell her she's lucky to live with the drinks guy, but really it's the drinks guy who's the lucky one.

INDEX

Note: Page numbers in *italics* refer to illustrations.

About the Author

Adam McDowell is a journalist and writer who lives in Toronto, Canada. He has written about drinks for the *National Post*, a major Canadian newspaper, since 2006; his weekly column is now on its third name (it's currently called "Fix My Drink"). He's also the resident booze expert for *The Social*, a popular daytime lifestyle show on North American television. You can follow his adventures at adam mcdowell.com, or on Twitter or Instagram at @a_mcdo.